My Life at Grey Gardens

My Life at Grey Gardens

13 Months and Beyond

A True and Factual Book

Lois Wright

ISBN-10: 0-9777462-1-6
ISBN-13: 978-0-9777462-1-7

Front cover painting: Lois Wright
Front cover photo: Dana Mueller
Back cover photos: collection of Lois Wright

Dedication

Dedicated to the Memory of
Edith "Big Edie" Bouvier Beale.

Edith Ewing Bouvier Beale
1895 – 1977

ACKNOWLEDGEMENTS

Deep appreciation to the late Rena Jackson, a great help, who placed this book in the Library of Congress and had it copyrighted in 1978. Rena was a friend of Little Edie Beale, Doris Francisco, and me.

I also want to thank my good friends, Andrew Afram and Andrew Mroczek, for their enthusiastic dedication to *My Life at Grey Gardens: 13 Months and Beyond.* Their devotion to the memories of Big Edith Bouvier Beale and her daughter Little Edie Bouvier Beale illustrates their loyalty to the fans of *Grey Gardens* and to those who will learn about the Beales through this book. Without the Andrews' help, I could never have managed to maneuver an old bulky manuscript from a box in a closet to a clean, fresh printed copy that can finally reach *Grey Gardens* fans.

Lois Wright

FOREWORD

Edith Bouvier Beale and her daughter Edie, known colloquially as Big Edie and Little Edie, were the aunt and cousin of former U.S. First Lady Jacqueline Bouvier Kennedy Onassis. They led an unconventional existence in Grey Gardens, a mansion in East Hampton near the ocean. The house was surrounded on the outside by overgrown gardens and filled on the inside with fleas, cats, raccoons, and old cans and rubbish. News of the Beales' living quarters first made local headlines, then regional headlines, and within months they had been cover stories on tabloid newspapers and had received attention by the international press.

Documentary filmmakers David and Albert Maysles brought cameras into the Beales' home and made the film *Grey Gardens*. The film not only showed how the Beales lived, but it introduced audiences to the Beales themselves, their manner of speaking, dressing, and their passions, interests, and dreams. The film developed a cult following and turned the Beales into bohemian heroines. The Beales, especially Little Edie, hold firm positions in popular culture. They have been depicted on the stage, top fashion designers have used them as inspiration in their collections, and quotations from the film have been incorporated into pop songs.

Lois Wright is the sole surviving Grey Gardens insider. Dr. John F. Erdmann, Lois's great uncle on her mother's side, owned a large summer home near Grey Gardens on the ocean side of Lily Pond Lane. A successful surgeon, Erdmann's expertise was once requested by President Grover Cleveland. As a young girl, Lois visited her uncle's home during the summers. She has lived in East Hampton since the age of twelve, but was educated privately in Manhattan.

Where the Maysles got to know the Beales over the course of their filming, Lois knew the Beales as long as she can remember. Like the Beales, she is an artist. Her spirituality and beliefs strongly coincide with those of the Beales, and she understands their wants, needs, and motivations. The Beales had always been a part of Lois's life, and when Lois's own mother died, Big Edie became like a second mother to Lois. After Big Edie died, Little Edie lived at Grey Gardens for two more years before moving to various new locations, and she and Lois corresponded until Edie's death in 2002.

This book is based on a manuscript that Lois wrote in the late 1970s from material she logged in journals kept from 1975 through 1977. It chronicles the time she lived at Grey Gardens with the Beales, and the months following that time, including Big Edie's passing. Lois's manuscript was a labor of love; she feels very strongly that the history of Grey Gardens should be preserved.

Lois has updated her original manuscript with more information gleaned from her journals, and has taken the opportunity to provide some previously missing information that will be of interest to members of the *Grey Gardens* fan community.

One of the most striking revelations found in this book is the Beales' response to negative press about their lives and the film. Although not specifically intended to serve as a defense of the Beales or the film, this book shows how absolutely at ease they were with their style of living, and their anger at critics who, perhaps with the intention of protecting the Beales, insulted and criticized them.

Beneath its sensational aspects, the film *Grey Gardens* presents the wonderfully unique relationship between a mother and daughter, while Lois's manuscript depicts the unconventional, playful relationship of an informal family of three artists. This book is a testament to the remarkable, exceptional lives of Big and Little Edie Beale, and to Lois Wright herself, the artist whose personal stories and remembrances have not been available to the general public.

Andrew Mroczek and Andrew Afram
"Big Andrew" and "Little Andrew"

Contents

My Life at Grey Gardens

Introduction

At Grey Gardens, the world cannot intrude. I feel it to be as safe and private as any mountain peak in ancient Tibet. With no formality of conduct, convention, or customs, the old house slowly envelops my mind and soul like a soft cocoon. Some day, as with Little Edie, I may turn into a special butterfly, but I don't. I look forward to a transformation, and not to old age or death. Perhaps this is one of the secrets of Grey Gardens: the desire to remain there until it's time. However, time seems not to exist, and the cats watch with interest. They seem to wait also. Only the raccoons live in reality, in the now.

Here, there is no hurry; there are no plans to act on. As Little Edie said, "It's very difficult to keep the line between the past and the present," and the future is expected to reveal a coming revelation of something important about it all, but it never seems to, and we living there do not really care.

Upstairs, Big Edie may have all the answers, and they are secure with her. I don't need to probe; it will all come, it's all so eternal.

I arrived with my green canvas stretcher-cot and other things on May 7th, 1975, and I lived day and night without interruption at Grey Gardens for 13 months, until June 25th, 1976. After that, I remained in East Hampton and continued a personal, close contact with the Beales and I still do, although our contact now is totally spiritual. They had a life force not to be underestimated! I will end this narrative after Big Edie's funeral on February 8th, 1977.

I enjoyed both Big and Little Edie so much and I miss them. I am writing this because it's time to. The Beales' unusual lives should not be forgotten! They were brave, colorful, talented people. Their spirit gets around.

I was no stranger to Grey Gardens. I had been there before, often, so I knew what to bring. A cot, blankets, cooking pots, food, flash light, a heavy stick or club, a hat or two, some dishes, what would be needed on most safaris, except a cap gun as I didn't have a real pistol. The Beales had a cap gun in Big Edie's room to frighten burglars and tourists away from the house.

Big Edie mentioned that "at night, cats, ghosts, rats, heavens only knows what—perhaps a gorilla—walked through the house" and to keep my door bolted, as they bolted their door every evening. Of course, a few raccoons might be around, but they seemed to go to sleep around 10:00 PM, unless something bothered them. Little Edie never gave me a lock of any kind for the door, but I guess it didn't bother me, as I slept like a log on my canvas stretcher.

Little Edie mentioned burglars and bombers and "last but not least of the dangers: Peter Beard." The Beales thought that whenever he was in East Hampton, he dropped off some strange animal from one of his recent trips from Africa to Montauk. We could certainly expect whatever creature he left on the property to soon find its way into the house and settle down.

Later, I brought all my paintings, as I never live in any place with out the faces I have painted. I soon needed my easel, and a couple of trunks, an old seaman's chest and some cardboard boxes to keep things in, as I didn't want my belongings out in the open. I managed to hang some clothes on another easel I had. After that, I gradually became "the ghost of Grey Gardens."

The Beale movie had expected to have its world premiere in N.Y.C. at the Lincoln Center on February 20, 1976 and Little Edie wanted me to stay out of sight. The Beales lived upstairs, except when Little Edie came downstairs to talk with me or to watch me paint. Only David and Al Maysles knew I was living there, and Big Edie's son, Bouvier, knew of my hidden existence in the upstairs room and kitchen-studio. My painting covered the walls where I lived.

Four giant loaves of fresh bread tossed out the upstairs hall window every afternoon at 4:00 PM. I thought they looked quite pleased carrying them away. When an unknown tourist-fan left food on the front porch for the Beales, the raccoons always benefited by it as Little Edie thought it might be poisoned and gave it to the raccoons, but it never was. All the raccoons led by Buster were very healthy and of normal activity. The cats were quite different.

The "icebox room" is in-between the kitchen and dining room, and wearing a hat there is a good idea. The raccoons are always staring down from large gaps in the ceiling and they can get carried away with curiosity and fall down. In fact, some of them jumped down at night. Little Edie had said that "any day now, Buster, the big, intelligent, old one of the group, would learn how to open the refrigerator door and that wouldn't help the grocery bill as we already spend too much on their food."

Little Edie and her mother thought the raccoons should be fed at a certain time each day, or else there would be big trouble! All the raccoons would attack in anger and tear the house down! I don't know how Buster had transmitted this demand to the Beales, but it worked.

But instead of being worried about all this, it seemed to add to the security, the feeling of being safe. A paradox, another Grey Gardens mystery. I do not know that if anything unpleasant was met in the halls between the bathroom and the kitchen, or any place. All you had to do was stand there with your stick and call Big Edie. She would handle it as she handled all the problems. Instructions would be given with firm dispatch, and Little Edie would dash out of her mother's room ready for battle, followed by her cats. Afterward, we all felt great, even if Little Edie said she wanted to leave Grey Gardens. Big Edie, the cats, and I knew she didn't.

Sometimes we could not find the cause of a loud noise that woke everyone, and Little Edie and I would go downstairs with our cap guns and a flashlight to hunt for a burglar or bomber. We were not frightened as we realized that Big Edie would watch over us from upstairs.

One night, the Beales were awake because of a pounding noise over their bedroom. I got up to investigate. Little Edie said an upset raccoon was pounding on their ceiling with a hammer. He was in the attic and I could hear it. Big Edie, from her bed, pounded back on the ceiling with her stick, while Little Edie just looked upwards. The raccoon stopped.

The Edith Bouvier Beales always protected their private life. They were, after all, famous recluses, and intended to live their solitary existence, be it scandalous or incredible, or dull or exciting.

The First Days, May 1975

Wednesday, May 7, 1975

I had a milkshake and a hamburger before I arrived at the Beales' at 5:30 PM with my cot and blankets and a few suit cases. The Beales and I talked for a bit, and then I was shown to my room.

I was given the "Eye of the House" room, which we called the "Eye Room" for short. It is upstairs and overlooks the front porch. I would end up staying downstairs most of the time, though.

I unfolded the canvas cot in my room and shortly retired. The room was hot and stuffy, as Edie had left heat on for the kittens and I couldn't open the windows. They were nailed closed, but some air came in from broken frames and glass. I slept well.

Thursday, May 8, 1975

I awoke in the morning to the pleasant hum of voices in Big Edie's room and the smell of bacon coming from their room. It's not a good idea to wear a long robe in Grey Gardens because of the floors, so I dressed, put my hat on to protect my head from raccoons, picked up my flashlight to see the way down the dark back stairs, and then I went through the "storage room" and arrived in the bright kitchen.

There are windows in the kitchen. I wouldn't need the club until evening, I thought. However, there were mornings I did need the club.

I started the water boiling for coffee on the little gas stove that Little Edie wouldn't use, and took a couple of slices of bread out of the metal box as nothing could be left out. Above all, the bar soap had to be kept in a can with a tight lid. Something in the house adored soap, and if I left the room for only a few minutes, it would disappear. Some kind of animal intended to keep clean, it would seem. Or, one of the real ghosts of Grey Gardens delighted in removing the Ivory Soap bar. Big Edie told me that Tom "Tex" Logan liked scissors and would usually take them, later returning the scissors to another room. Poor Tom died in the kitchen in 1964 and I attended his burial with Little Edie on a cold winter day. We were the only ones there except for Reverend Davis. Anyway, I knew Little Edie liked scissors also, so I tried to keep them "under cover" in my room.

I managed to close the door from the icebox room and returned to the stove when Little Edie scraped and pushed the door open again with much energy to determine what I was doing. Edie liked to "check up" as she said, and then report "the Beale office" discoveries to her mother. I was always glad to see Edie, as she possessed such an "alive" quality.

I asked Little Edie not to scrape the door open with so much energy, as it was ready to fall off the hinges. Little Edie ignored that and said in a stage whisper, "Lois, do you think it's safe to plug the refrigerator in? You can if you want." I replied that I didn't know and suggested that she do it. Little Edie, still whispering, said, "It's Brooks's icebox you know. Mother bought it for him for $30 and it might set the house of fire."

Little Edie was dressed in her "coat-vest," a brown leather coat with the sleeves cut out, a gift from Mr. Onassis. The usual scarf was well-placed on her head. She looked well. "Do you think Brooks will call us? Mother wants him for some repair work in her room. I hope he phones. I will keep the cats out of your bathroom, Lois, dear, did you know that the bathroom was on TelStar just after the raid? Oh God, that raid. If only I knew who started it, I would sue them for two million dollars. It ruined my mother's health." Little Edie's voice changed from the soft whisper to a much louder tone, and glaring at me said, "Did you do it? Perhaps you were the one!"

I smiled, "No, Edie."

"Well then, it was my brother, or the L.V.I.S, or Nixon."

At that moment, the downstairs pantry phone rang, next to the icebox room.

"It's mother," Edie said. "She needs something, I better answer."

"Hello, Mother? Yes, yes, Lois is drinking coffee. Yes, she used the stove! I'll be right up."

Edie plugged the refrigerator in and left the icebox room swiftly for her mother's bedroom via the front stairway.

Later, I went up to say good morning to Big Edie and talk for a few minutes. We didn't chat long, as we all had so much we wanted to do. Big Edie was busy in her bed washing out the new kittens' eyes, and Edie had to help her heat some warm water on the electric hot plate, and I felt like moving some boxes around in my room and also wanted to see if I could get some more air.

I went into my room and pushed some window frames out to allow for larger opened spaces. A trusting raccoon sitting on the front porch roof pushed his black nose through a hole in the glass window to sniff at me. Just then, Pinky and Whiskers, two favorite cats, appeared on the roof and started to fight. The raccoon withdrew his snoot, climbed down under the roof somewhere. I called Little Edie as Pinky and Whiskers fell off the roof locked in combat. Edie ran downstairs and out the front door. She brought Pinky up in her arms.

"I am going to have Whiskers before the firing squad," Little Edie said. "He started it, poor Pinky." Pinky was another male, but no match for Whiskers, as he was part Coon cat, with huge green eyes. He wanted to rule, but one look from Black Cat, Big Edie's favorite male, and Whiskers would stop his nonsense. Black Cat would lie on the wide banister railing looking like a Sphinx from Egypt. In the summer, he slept there all night. Black cat never took his eyes off me whenever I walked past. One evening, he came into a dream I had and gossiped about all the other cats.

The cats, like Grey Gardens, may always remain a riddle.

The Rest of May 1975

Friday, May 9, 1975

This afternoon, I decided to leave Grey Gardens for the grocery store. The Beales ordered their provisions from The Newtown, and they delivered every day, but I thought it better to get my own food. I wanted to avoid any confusion regarding their monthly bills. Big Edie liked to give me a candy bar once in a while, but that is all I ever accepted. If I hadn't taken it, Big Edie said she would "never speak to [me] again!"

I met Little Edie in the upstairs hall, and she said, "Where are you going? Look at that hat! It looks like the Orient. Listen, Lois, I'm getting out of this place! I'm going to Florida or France. You can take over. Get it?!"

"No, Edie, it takes four people to do what you do here."

"Thanks, old kid."

"Let me out, will you? I told your mother I wanted to go to the store now; she knows I want to leave."

"When will you be back? I have to lock you out."

"In about an hour. Come on, Edie, let's go downstairs, come on…"

Big Edie called from her room, "Edie! Edie! Don't be too long. I want to go out on the porch, right now, not next week!"

"All right, Mother. Lois wants to go out!"

Little Edie and I walked down the back stairs and into the kitchen. After unlocking the back door and the screen door, I turned and said, "Now, don't forget, when I return, I will call from outside, under Big Edie's window. What if you are asleep or something?"

"I never sleep! Mother will hear you anyway."

"I like your head scarf."

"Oh, thanks; it's an old sweater." Edie smiled.

The pantry phone started to ring. I knew it was Big Edie. Her phone was right next to the bed. She couldn't walk now and used a small red leather and chrome rolling chair called a "run-about" that my mother had before she died. I brought it over to her months ago after she had called me to see if I could locate a large tricycle for her. I knew she didn't want to use a depressing and unattractive wheelchair. I had managed to get it in my Karmann Ghia and Little Edie and I carried it up the front stairs together.

I dashed out of Grey Gardens so that Little Edie could go back upstairs after latching everything against the intruders.

I did my shopping quickly and was anxious to return home.

Big Edie heard me calling right away. She always heard me and answered within seconds. I can recall her lovely voice… "Edie! Edie! It's Lois. She wants to come in. Yes, it's Lois… hurry up! What are you doing? Edie!"

I was let in by Little Edie and relieved to be back inside. The town was getting crowded.

I found all the lights out upstairs. Big Edie had phoned for an electrician. He would be here tomorrow morning. It didn't matter; I had my flashlight and some candles. The Beales' electric double hot plate was off, so they were using Sterno. I went down into the kitchen and cooked my dinner on the gas stove. They didn't want to be bothered about it, I knew. Big Edie loved using the Sterno. She was an expert with it, even in her bed.

I called good night on my way to the Eye Room and the Beales answered through their locked door. "Don't use a candle," Little Edie hollered. "You might burn the house down!"

Sunday, May 11, 1975

MOTHER'S DAY

David Maysles stopped by in the morning, and about 6:00 PM, as expected, Bouvier Beale and his son arrived from Bridgehampton. They were allowed into Big Edie's room.

Little Edie offered her brother and nephew some soup from a can. It was expensive soup. Bouvier smiled, looked at me, and said, "How about a nice bowl of botulism?"

No one had any soup except Little Edie and her mother. A little singing went on, and then the guests were locked out the front door.

We all gave Big Edie gifts, and Little Edie made a card for her.

Monday, May 12, 1975

I didn't finish the page in my log book, therefore I don't know why I wrote this. "Felt a Presence in my room tonight." Perhaps I didn't care to describe it.

Monday, May 19, 1975

JOHN VERNOU BOUVIER III'S BIRTHDAY

I was hanging about ten of my paintings in the kitchen, when Little Edie scrapped the door open and said, "Oh, Lois, I always wondered what would be on the walls, they look just right here. I used to thumbtack pictures from magazines on them, but they disappeared after The Raid. Colored pictures of vegetables and things. By the way, Mother wants to see you upstairs." Edie laughed.

I put down my Grandmother's hammer and left for Big Edie's room. Big Edie, in bed, looked at me. "Your jacket should be more fitted, like the French. A beautiful morning, I should be out on the upstairs porch now, but I haven't had an extra minute! Edie took too long cooking breakfast. Have you had your coffee?"

"Oh yes. I was hanging paintings."

"I know. Lois, it's May 19th, my brother Jack's birthday, and I think Jacqueline must have sent a hundred dollars worth of flowers to her father's grave. Don't you think so?"

"Well, it's possible…"

"Will you drive there now and bring all the flowers back here? I think we should enjoy them, and Jack wouldn't care. We could put some downstairs in the entrance hall."

"My car isn't working too well. I wouldn't want to get stranded in the cemetery with Jacqueline's flowers in my car. You know, it's way out of town."

"Don't do it, then. What is wrong with your little car?"

"It makes me nervous… stalls, trouble starting, and the brakes hardly work."

"You need another car."

"I know that."

"When the movie profits come in, I'll buy a Rolls Royce that we can all use."

Little Edie opened the door. "Oh, Mother, a Cadillac would be fine! But I haven't decided on the color. God! Don't send Lois to the cemetery! She might get raped if she can't get out, and then she would sue us."

"I would not sue, Edie!"

Big Edie noticed a kitten. "Don't do that, Kitty. Don't do that! Kitty… come over here."

The kitten was ready to settle down on the hot-plate and Little Edie had a pan ready to warm milk. There were kittens all over the bed, including the gray-striped mother cats.

"Feed the males, Edie, or there's going to be a fight!"

"Oh, Mother, I know what I'm doing."

"Well," I said, "I'm going back downstairs. I am sorry about the flowers."

"Poor Jack... it's his birthday." Big Edie looked sad.

"Mother! He was too French, all the aspects... I won't go into all that now, but... I'm a *Beale*. I know *my* way around."

"Yes, around the Moon."

Edie smiled. "I could have been a great lawyer if I hadn't wanted to dance. I studied in my Father's office, the Beale office."

"You can't dance in court, you know." Big Edie started to sing... and Little Edie poured the warm milk into a dish. "Over here, kitty, I think some of them are Pinky's." Little Edie looked pleased. "They are Pinky's!"

"He screws all the time... why not?" Big Edie said pleasantly.

We named Pinky's two kittens Pinky One and Pinky Two.

Thursday, May 22, 1975

Nothing eventful happened, except the animals in the house made a great deal of noise last night. Or was it the animals, since I couldn't see them? In a deserted room next to my bedroom, it sounded like a mattress being pushed or slid across the floor. Edie said, "It must have been the raccoons getting comfortable, Lois, darling." The odd noise didn't really bother me, I just wondered, then turned over in my stretcher, and went back to sleep. It seemed almost impossible not to rest well in Grey Gardens.

Friday, May 23, 1975

THE MEMORIAL DAY WEEK-END

I helped Little Edie remove all the large black plastic garbage bags of trash from the hall near my bathroom, down the back steps into the kitchen, and then out the back door and through the outside room—it was composed of hedges—and past the driveway and onto the Lily Pond Lane area near the road. It wasn't easy. You had to work fast because Little Edie didn't want to leave the door unlocked more than a few minutes; she thought someone might try to sneak in the house. The trash men arrived on Mondays and Fridays. The slippery bags were heavy with cat food cans, milk cans, all the wet newspapers from Big Edie's bedroom floor, I don't know what all… They were extremely heavy; Little Edie always carried the impossible ones.

Big Edie had rolled into the upstairs porch room about 8:00 AM, followed by all the cats. Little Edie had pushed the "rolling chair", sometimes I pushed it, and sometimes Big Edie moved it along by herself. The cats liked the change, and Big Edie believed the air and sun would benefit them. She loved to be on the upstairs porch. It wasn't screened, right out in the open and over the neglected Italian garden below and the thick green jungle you couldn't penetrate. In the distance, the ocean could be seen. It all seemed like another world… even the telephone didn't intrude in this safe, independent, and happy place. The many kittens provided the amusement for Big Edie, and she enjoyed them. There were a few too many flies and bees to suit me, but they didn't bother the Beales. Big Edie kept her eyes on an old straw carrying bag that she brought with her. It remained next to her at all times. She locked the bedroom after leaving, but this was so important, it had to remain with her. I never noticed Big Edie opening it except to get out her checkbook. I didn't ask what the bag contained, and she never mentioned the subject, only would say, "Get my bag, Edie; I'm going on the porch… Edie!" Once in a while, she would ask me to bring it, as she watched. I never really thought about it then, but sometimes now, I do wonder…

Saturday, May 24, 1975

This morning, Brooks Hires arrived in his old red car. He had been working for the Beales off and on since the raid at Grey Gardens by the Suffolk County Health Dept. in 1971. Big Edie had been paying him with money that the Maysles had given her when she signed their contract to film a documentary movie that later would be named "Grey Gardens". Brooks, a good looking black man, around 40 years old, had simply arrived alone one day and managed to see Little Edie cutting the grass. Now, he worked inside the house also, cleaning the floors and plugging up rat holes and whatever Big Edie wanted. He was a great help.

The Maysles gave Brooks $10 and "shot" him cutting the grass. At that time, he worked mostly outside.

I was given $300 for my appearance in the movie. Big Edie insisted that I drive over and appear in the film. Little Edie frowned on this, but was overruled.

I was sitting in the kitchen when Little Edie dashed in. "Lois… can you call Brooks, Mother wants to see him right away before he starts on the grass. I'll let you out while you call him. He's way off by the Lily Pond Lane entrance."

"Brooks… Oh, Brooks!"

"Yes, Miss Lois?"

"Mrs. Beale wants to talk with you."

"All right," Brooks said, as he took off his white pith helmet and headed for the back porch.

Little Edie unlocked the door and allowed us in. I felt like I had accomplished something.

"All right."

After Brooks had closed the hall door, Edie whispered, "Isn't he good looking? An ex-athlete from Florida, raised by the nuns. I could go for him... if it weren't for Mr. Krug's ghost."

Mr. Krug is Julius "Cap" Krug, who was the Secretary of Interior in President Truman's cabinet. Cap had died years ago, and Little Edie had asked me to do an oil portrait of him. She "never got over" Cap.

"Well," Little Edie's voice changed to a commanding level. "I better get back upstairs before Brooks steals something. Mother is just too trusting... She's a Bouvier." Little Edie hurried up the back steps.

I looked at the small newspaper clippings of Mr. Krug, a heavy man, 300 pounds, Little Edie said. I hoped that his spirit would assist me to paint his Earthly image, I felt that he would. About a week later, I knew that Cap had, as Little Edie really liked the portrait, and I felt him by my side as I painted. I think Edie was a little jealous of his presence with me in the kitchen, or "studio," as Little Edie called the room now.

Little Edie holds my painting of Cap on the
front porch of Grey Gardens.

Sunday, May 25, 1975

From my view out of the leaded pane windows of the Eye Room, I noticed another familiar car drive into the West End Road driveway, at the front of Grey Gardens. There were not many familiar cars, only two, and the grocery store van. Was it the Maysles brothers? No, it was David Maysles and his wife Judy. They parked and got out of their car and started calling for the Beales, and knocking on the wide green front door.

"Oh, God!" Little Edie shouted. "What do they want? I'll go see what they are up to now! Lois... You watch Judy; you can't be too careful with a woman snooping around, promise me! Make absolutely certain they don't let a cat out. One of them would drive off with it."

I agreed to the instructions, and after a while, Little Edie's film producer and Judy were nervously given permission to enter. Edie would rather David had arrived alone, or with Al.

Of course, Big Edie was on the alert, and calling to her daughter not to stay downstairs forever.

I positioned myself in the upstairs hall where I could watch the activity, and at the same time report to Big Edie. It wasn't too long before we were all in Big Edie's room.

The visit turned out to be just a social call. No news about the film release, just the three women editors in New York City, still slaving over the nearly one hundred hours of filming. The movie had to be cut to about an hour and a half!

David and Judy shortly left for Montauk. David and Al Maysles had rented a small cottage in Southampton for the summer, but they all knew friends in Montauk.

Later, I drove slowly into town and found it to be most difficult, Memorial Day parade on Main St. It was awful. I returned to Grey Gardens where it seemed "as quiet as the tomb" as if no animals, humans, or ghosts existed in the old house. What were they doing? Sleeping, meditating... Naturally, I did a great deal of meditating and it was a peaceful time. Soon the parade racket of noisy confusion receded from my mind.

Thursday, May 29, 1975

Mary Hedges phoned to ask me to read palms at a party in Wainscott in July, at an interesting house built right on the dunes. It was owned and occupied by two wealthy men. The Beales were delighted with my hand analysis work, and I needed and wanted to do it for extra cash. I feel that the hands are a blueprint of the person. I agreed to go, after asking Little Edie if she would stay awake that night to let me back into Grey Gardens. Little Edie said she would, as she knew there would also be a few dollars for her.

So far, since I have been living here, Little Edie hasn't left the property. If she had, then I would be the one to lock her out, and reopen the door upon her return.

JUNE 1975

Monday, June 2, 1975

Stove gas delivered this morning. Big Edie ordered it as I had informed her that the stove was dead. She paid cash for it, but charged a few items at the East Hampton Hardware Store to Jacqueline Onassis. Among the inexpensive things, a floor mat had to be placed in front of the stove, as the floor seemed to be sinking there. I had to stand very lightly or off to one side whenever I cooked. The kitchen-studio really needed a new floor, or repair work. The little black square rubber mat just had "to do."

The great, huge old iron coal stove named "Perfection" was on another side of the room, but it couldn't be used since the raid. Little Edie used to lug bags of coal up from the basement for it. Big Edie had once enjoyed cooking on the antique.

This afternoon, I brought the Beales in some ice cream from the I.G.A. where I shopped. They loved ice cream and so did I. However, we couldn't keep it in reserve, as the freezer in the refrigerator didn't work. Also, no ice cubes.

I had also bought some fish cakes and gave Little Edie half of them to heat on their hot-plate.

Friday, June 6, 1975

Little Edie mentioned today that David had phoned, and will arrive tomorrow. I think his visit must have something to do with Big Edie signing a will form that their lawyer, Tommy Epstein, sent her from New York City. Big Edie will need three people to witness. Without the Maysles, it would be impossible, since no one is allowed into Big Edie's room. Of course, I would be the first witness to sign. I expected the proceedings to be emotional, and there seemed to be an electric excitement upstairs.

This morning, while I was folding up my stretcher and placing it on all the boxes of top of a rusty bedspring that served as a platform for them, Little Edie came in and informed me that "Al Maysles will arrive with David tonight for the will signing," and to "be ready!"

Later, they arrived, but Big Edie wasn't ready. It was a really uneventful evening. The filmmakers brought their equipment for a few projects.

Sunday, June 8, 1975

The Maysles arrived with an attractive woman photographer named Marianne Barcellona. They set up lights and cameras in the porch room to take stills of Little Edie. Big Edie wouldn't leave her room and refused to sign the will. I spent most of my time telling Big Edie what they were doing. Little Edie became The Star once again, and posed for many pictures. Later, David obtained our dinner from Chez Labbat restaurant and we ate chicken in the upstairs hall. After that, I drove Marianne to the railroad station and returned home.

David asked me to say "good-bye" about ten times on his movie tape recorder. It was all film work. The Maysles even went through the unused rooms downstairs, recording the silence, or any odd sounds that might be heard. I wondered if anything would be slinking around, but the house was quiet, as if the old mansion knew the long felt-covered mic was invading an inner, secret atmosphere. We couldn't talk while they were doing this, couldn't even "tip toe."

Monday, June 9, 1975

The Maysles arrived again today and continued their work with Little Edie. They were just correcting some technical matters for their studio people.

I brought in some ice cream for Big Edie, as I thought she would need it before the will business started.

Another hour and we would all be gathered in Big Edie's room for the signing. The right moment came at last, and before anything happened, David set up his tape recorder and turned it on. He asked Big Edie to read the entire will out loud and she proceeded to. Then she signed: Edith Ewing Bouvier Beale. Little Edie suddenly jumped from the chair and seemed to be almost overcome. She shouted, "Oh, Mother… My darling Mother!" and "This reminds me of Cap!" and then she started to cry softly. Why this reminded her of Cap, no one knew. I suggested brandy, well aware we didn't have any, but it did seem the correct thing to offer. Little Edie politely declined. A death bed scene, except for Big Edie. She was calm and concentrating on what she was doing.

About a half hour later, we all marched out so that Big Edie could rest from the dramatic activity. Even the cats seemed impressed and had stopped their "screwing" to watch with interest.

The Maysles were soon locked out of the front door by Little Edie, who had started to whisper about what a sad ordeal it had been.

Big Edie seemed in good health, except for the fact she couldn't walk. It was just that Big Edie wanted to decide on the fate of Grey Gardens, in The Year of Our Lord 1975 on a June 9th evening. She didn't want her home all "chopped up" if something ever happened to her.

Tuesday, June 10th, 1975

David and Al Maysles back in New York City now. They phoned the Beales from there. Will return here in two weeks. More film work, no doubt.

Wednesday, June 11, 1975

I talked with Big and Little Edie on the upstairs porch this morning. They seemed to want me to be there. I had the feeling something important should be said, perhaps by Big Edie, but the conversation really didn't amount to anything. Big Edie showed me a picture of Jacqueline, and then I retreated from the Grey Gardens bees. They also love the outdoor porch. Little Edie ignored them, as she ignored all insects, flies, and even cat dirt, lying face up on the deck boards. Only the fleas would cause her to lash out in irritation. "I can't go through another summer with the God damn hedge fleas. Don't open a window, Lois, or I will ask you to leave, don't you dare, when my back is turned! They invade, and get all over the house! Tell her, Mother!"

Big Edie answered, "Oh, shut up, Edie. Open the upstairs hall window before I hit you with this cane!" she said pleasantly.

Little Edie snickered at her Mother and squinted her eyes.

"Go on, get up and let some air in the hall. You want to suffocate my cats? I don't want my kittens to die! Edie! Do it; open that window!"

By this time, I was on my way down the back stairs. I knew the dreaded fleas didn't come from the tall hedges; they came from within the house. I couldn't open the Eye Room windows anyway, but I did open the kitchen-studio door to allow air in when Little Edie was upstairs. The cats' greatest enemy was the fleas, then the raccoons. Both were killers.

I wondered about the vibrations on the porch earlier, mostly from Big Edie. Once in a while this mysterious something would hang in the atmosphere.

Friday, June 13, 1975

FRIDAY THE 13TH

A heavy rain all day. It was really quite a storm, and we also had strong winds off the ocean. Large pots and pans were placed here and there in the house wherever the ceilings dripped water. The rain was coming in my room, too, but it couldn't harm the floor. I would place thick newspapers down and they would absorb the rainwater. After a few days, I removed them.

Outside, small lakes were forming on the grounds and the front driveway turned to soft mud. The grocery truck would have to park in the street and the poor delivery boy had to walk in with the cardboard carton of items ordered by Big Edie. Never a small amount, not with all the animals.

However, I found it restful, and the many cats enjoyed the weather also. Big Edie liked to hear the rain; Little Edie called it a hurricane and would get excited. She was dressed in bright red today, even her head scarf. Little Edie reminded me of a Gypsy. She moved like one and adored dancing to Spanish music.

The feline smell was powerful in the old house now, living here I didn't care. It was a good Friday the 13th.

I had time to think over the unusual telephone calls the Beales were receiving. They were talking with someone frequently. Who could it be? I knew it wasn't the Maysles. Whoever it was, Big and Little Edie were secret about the person's identity, so I couldn't ask, or ever appear that I knew "something was going on." They dialed some of the calls, very odd…

I decided to forget about it and write in my logbook. It would soon be time for lunch, a peanut butter sandwich in the kitchen-studio.

Little Edie entered. "Lois, don't unlock the back door! A maniac could get in and kill my mother. Do you want her death on your hands? He might murder all of us. God! I have to watch everything! Do you think just because the screen doors locked, that's going to stop him?"

"I'll leave the wooden door closed."

It was too cool anyway.

Wednesday, June 18, 1975

I painted today, a small blue canvas to meditate by. An eye within a larger eye. I had just completed it when Little Edie arrived from upstairs. With her long graceful strides, she moved quickly over to the easel.

"Oh, Lois, I do like it… why it's the Beale eyes!"

"No, Edie, I don't think so…"

"Oh, *yes*! It's the right shade of blue. I *know*! Could I have it? When the Maysles pay Mother and me, I'll buy it from you. I would like to hang it in my room now…"

"After the paint dries."

I doubted that I would ever see it again. First, Big Edie would agree regarding Little Edie's intention to hang it, and then, as with my other oils Edie liked, it would disappear into Grey Gardens, swallowed by some part of the house. Occasionally, one or two were regurgitated, much to my surprise, and appeared to be in excellent condition. If a painting was hung in the halls of "living room," then it was safe, but not if the destination was Little Edie's room.

Little Edie was pleased with her acquisition. I put down my brushes. "Now look, Edie, that's to meditate by, take care of it."

Edie glared. "Don't you think I know how to save things? Haven't I been taking care of my Mother's possessions for years? She's a collector, but would have lost everything without me! I'm always on the job, kiddo."

"Then where are your mother's blue slippers?!"

"Don't be silly... I can't watch Brooks every second."

"Edie! Oh, *Edie!*" Hearing Big Edie's voice, there was a moment of silence until Little Edie said, "Oh, I have to feed the cats, that's what I came down for, to get some milk. Mother will kill me for taking so long. I'm coming right up, Mother!"

The pantry phone started to ring and I answered it. "Hello?"

"Oh, hello, Lois. Please tell Edie to come immediately. The cats are hungry, they need their dinner. I called Edie but she didn't answer. Oh... here she is now. Stop that, Pinky! Edie! A kitten just fell off the bed, pick it up... No... It's over there... Can't you see it? Put it back with the mother cat. What's the matter with you, the kitten is by your foot... turn around. Good-bye, Lois."

"Good-bye." I started to place the receiver down.

"Oh, Lois, stop by my room in about an hour. I have a candy bar for you. Now, don't forget. I saved it for you, it's on my night table and I want you to have it!"

I thanked Big Edie and hung up. I didn't care about the candy bar, but I knew that Love went along with the gift. The candy seemed to be almost wrapped in a wonderful kindness that belonged to Big Edie. She shared it freely inside Grey Gardens with Little Edie and me.

Thursday, June 26, 1975

Little Edie was talking on the telephone. "Oh, hello, Al, darling... Do you really want to come at noon? Well... I'll try to be ready... Now, don't bring anyone with you! Just David... One of the editors, Muffie? God! Now I'll have to clean Mother's room... All right, Al... What I have to go through for this movie! I don't think it's worth it... Goodbye, Al."

David, Al, and Muffie Meyer arrived and were eventually let in. I became involved as David asked me to read Muffie's hands, but I only studied them a few minutes, as they were in the Eye Room looking around. David asked if I slept on the folding canvas stretcher and I said "yes." Didn't know why that should interest them. I pointed out my great grand mother's silver coffee urn from Kentucky. I wanted to remove their attention from various aspects of the room. I realized other people have beds, and perhaps they thought it odd that I didn't. There are no beds in Grey Gardens, except for the two in Big Edie's room. I preferred a canvas cot. It was better for the flea situation; however, I didn't bother to explain. Of course, my blankets were folded up inside a box and it appeared to them that I didn't have any. Little Edie was right, the Maysles were snooping around.

Later, the guests talked with Little Edie on the back porch, while I remained with Big Edie.

"What are they doing, Lois?"

"Chatting outside."

"Edie will loosen their ears permanently with her incessant chattering... Poor kitty... this one's not well and she should be taking care of it. Kept me awake all last night, wouldn't leave my chest for a minute. A beautiful little kitty… I need a chocolate milk, and it's time to feed the raccoons… Will you turn the light on, please?"

"Yes. The kitten seems to be getting more energy now."

"Better call Edie now… She could talk indefinitely."

I closed the door and went back down the back stairs with my flashlight guiding the way. It would also keep a rat from running at me.

Monday, June 30, 1975

Little Edie was standing by her Mother's door in the hall, and she had a worried expression.

"Good morning, Edie, what's the matter?!"

"Good morning, Lois. I think it's going to be a clear day. I want to get some sun. Did you hear the racket last night?"

"No, I didn't hear anything. What was it?"

"Just Buster in the attic, banging around. He's so heavy! I think it's their mating season. Could you mail this letter to Jackie certified? It will cost a dollar, but I have the money. A return receipt and a stamp. Could you mail it right away?"

"As soon as I get dressed and have breakfast. Would that be all right?"

"I guess so…" Little Edie gave me four quarters from a tiny silk purse. "I think it's worth a dollar, don't you? Jackie may not get it otherwise. Bring back the receipt! I don't trust that post office."

Little Edie didn't say what they had in the envelope. I decided it was an extra Grey Gardens bill or the usual electric bill that the Beales sent to Jacqueline. Whatever it was, I knew Little Edie was very late in sending it in. If we were dangerously close to having the lights turned off, then Big Edie would telephone the power company and save us until Nancy Tuckerman had written a check for Jacqueline Onassis and mailed it to them.

I placed the coins and the letter in my "wear in the house clothes" jacket, and left for the kitchen-studio.

Little Edie shouted after me, "Mother asked me to tell you to go directly to the post office before the mail goes out. I'll be right down to let you out! Let me know when you are ready to leave!"

"I will, Edie," I shouted back.

July & August 1975

Friday, July 4, 1975

INDEPENDENCE DAY

It was a quiet holiday here. I exchanged a few small gifts with the Beales. Big Edie had asked for two or three American flags from Marley's Stationery store on Main St. for the upstairs porch, and I had obtained them Thursday. Little Edie placed one in the entrance hall. It looked patriotic and peaceful. We could hear some fireworks from the Georgica beach.

After dinner, I left for Wainscott, and the party there. I expected to work hard reading palms, and I most certainly did. Everyone was interested and a long line of guests formed to wait in line to have their hands analyzed. I was situated in a special room in back of a huge telescope that overlooked the ocean on an observatory porch. The guests had to climb a cured iron, outdoor stairway to reach me. It was a lovely night, and "The Beautiful People" were in abundance. Somewhere below, a rock group played, two long bars had been set up, and, further back, the Mathew's house could be seen.

I drank ginger ale and concentrated on the lines and mounts and contours of all the hands.

I did wish that Little Edie could be here. She would have enjoyed dancing alone to the music, but I knew she wouldn't leave Grey Gardens. It was comforting to feel the Beales with me in their thoughts.

I returned home around midnight and noticed the front porch light bulb had been left on for me, and some downstairs lights. No doubt their flashlight was missing.

Big and Little Edie heard me calling under the windows and Little Edie opened the door right away. I went into Big Edie's room as she wanted to talk a few minutes about the party and make certain I had survived.

"Well, Lois, you didn't get murdered or kidnapped. You could have been killed!" Big Edie said.

Little Edie agreed. "You could have been in an accident on the trip back and died on the highway. Then... we would have your body to think about... and a funeral. God!"

Saturday, July 5, 1975

This afternoon, I gave Little Edie ten dollars from my fifty dollar check that I received last night. She snatched it quickly as any Gypsy would. "Don't tell Mother," she whispered.

It was a busy day. I had problems with the Ghia and I had bought a very old rather large U.S. mail truck. It needed work. Edie liked the truck.

Tuesday, July 8, 1975

Around 3:00 PM at the East Hampton post office, I rotated the dials on the Beales' locked box, and then opened the little gold door. Nothing too much except an envelope from 1040 Fifth, Jacqueline's address. I knew Big Edie would want it right away, so I left the building and climbed into the Ghia. It managed to start and I drove back to Main

St., and then down Lily Pond Lane. I moved the car in between the two old cement posts at the back entrance, parking near the Grey Gardens windows.

"Hello, Edie! Let me in! I'm back early!"

Big Edie answered, calling Little Edie, and I was admitted.

The note was from Nancy Tuckerman and the Beales read it out loud. It wasn't important. Jackie had just left for Europe. She wanted to thank her aunt and cousin for the flowers they sent at the time of Ari Onassis's funeral.

Big Edie liked Ari Onassis. She had met him via the telephone when he was in New York City with Jacqueline and had invited them to be guests at Grey Gardens. She had informed them that she knew "he liked singers" and proceeded to sing something for him. He then sang a song back to Big Edie and they had a good time on the phone. After that, he had very interesting leather clothes sent to the Beales. Also a dark blue blanket with a white anchor on it from his yacht. At Grey Gardens, it was always called "The Onassis Blanket."

Big Edie was sad about Ari's passing, as she had hoped he would visit here. He said on the phone that he would look forward to it. Perhaps it was a mistake that he never managed to. Big Edie might have cheered him up.

"Poor Ari," Little Edie said. "He would have loved Mother! We could have helped him over his depression after his son died."

"Where would Jacqueline and Mr. Onassis have slept?" I ventured.

"Oh, anywhere. In my brother's old room; it's quite large. Brooks could have mopped up in there, and then put brightly colored cushions on the floor for them. I don't really like beds; two mattresses would have been a good plan. Don't you think so, Mother?"

"Edie, I couldn't have so many people in the house. Just as well they didn't come. Get me a wet wash cloth for my hands."

"Mother can't stand confusion, but I could have handled them. Little goody two-shoes would have known what to do."

"Edie! How long are you going to make me wait for the wash cloth, until Christmas? Please stop that cat from screwing his sister… she's too young. Edie!"

I said good-bye, opened and shut the door quickly so that a kitten wouldn't run out into the hall. It would have been destroyed by the raccoons at night.

Wednesday, July 9, 1975

My Birthday

Birthdays at Grey Gardens are always a big event. When it is time to give gifts, Little Edie would go through her things to find something. One year, she gave me a pair of Caroline Kennedy's boots, as she thought they would fit. Big Edie would order a pair of slippers or slacks from Brill's, as she thought I needed them and the present would be gift-wrapped. My birthday was an important event, as it is also Big Edie's mother's birthday. Before I lived here, the Beales always managed to appear at my house for the occasion.

Thursday, July 17, 1975

David Maysles phoned and, after talking with the Beales, asked to speak with me. "Lois, do me a favor and paint another Masonite board to go with 'Big Edith Bouvier Beale—the Great Singer.' Paint 'Little Edith Bouvier Beale—the Great Dancer' instead of what we have, 'Little Edie Beale—the Great Star.' We will be down this weekend."

I had painted the two signs for the Beales as a birthday gift for Big Edie, and at the time, had no idea they would be in a movie. I just enjoyed doing them and thought they would make an excellent present.

I didn't want to paint another one for a film. However, Big Edie said she would ask David to give me fifty dollars for my efforts so I decided to do it. We could use the money. I found an old board and some paint, and started the background.

The Maysles didn't arrive this week-end. "Well, Al is in Alaska," Little Edie just told me.

Monday, July 21, 1975

At 10:00 PM, my usual time to retire, I went upstairs and into my room. I didn't care too much for the appearance of my floor. I had wet mopped it, but the floor really needed scraping, as it hadn't been cleaned properly in years and years and cats had been in here before I arrived. I never looked at the floor until it was "time to spread the newspapers," a procedure—almost a ritual—that I followed every evening. First, I picked up a stack of newspapers, walked over to where I would place my stretcher and then carefully spread them on the floor. I was generous, as I didn't want my one large sheet—folded lengthways—and blanket to touch anything except the papers. I unfolded the "cot", arranged it to my satisfaction and then slipped quickly between the sheet on the opened side, the other side of the sheet being folded. The canvas had become rather thin and it would have been upsetting if the material came loose from the light metal frame. Then… I would be reduced to sleeping on the floor.

About the time I got settled, the fleas were up from under the newspapers and hopping up and down, sounding like Mexican jumping beans. Ticky…ticky…tick.

I wore a soft linen hat with a wide brim on my head and pulled the sheet up to my chin. Ticky...tick... the fleas were getting quiet and would soon sleep also. Tick, tick.

If you got up at night, it woke the fleas and excited them, and you had to flick a few off, trying to return "inside" the sheet before more landed. I informed my body not to feel the need to go down the hall to the bathroom, as this gathered more fleas. It was only a summer problem; they disappeared when the cool weather arrived. As long as a burglar or a madman didn't break into Grey Gardens, I wouldn't have to get up and be bothered by the fleas.

I thought of the Beales. In Big Edie's room, the cats and kittens attracted the tiny things, and some cats died because of it. I had no animals in the Eye Room. Nevertheless, the fleas did get on you in Big Edie's room and sometimes they were still leaping off me in the post office. Only one or two, however.

Tuesday, July 22, 1975

Before I was off the stretcher this morning, Little Edie knocked on the door, and I said, "Come in."

"Oh, good morning, Lois. How did you sleep?"

"Fine. *Don't* let a cat in, *Edie!*"

"The mother cats like it in here. That one's going to have kittens."

"Now it going towards the chair... Catch her, Edie!"

"All right, but it wants to have her kittens here."

"*No...* someplace else!"

Little Edie picked up the gray-striped cat. "Mother wanted to ask you to buy something from White's Drug Store, when you go out."

"I will."

"Lois, why do you have all the newspapers on the floor? We have them for the cats to shit on. Pardon the expression." Edie laughed, "But you don't need them."

"Well, it keeps the dust down… and this 'cot' is low and I don't like everything all over the floor."

"Oh, God! The hedge fleas are terrible. But they'll die soon. It's almost fall. Mother wants some spray for them. I had to close the window last night; they were so annoying."

"You better open it now. Your Mother needs air."

"She's going on the porch. This entire house should be air conditioned and all the windows sealed tight. I wonder what it would cost…"

The mother cat was getting nervous. Little Edie opened my door to leave.

"Edie! Oh, *Edie*, I'm in the chair. I want to go out! Come on… stop talking to Lois so much."

Little Edie smiled and left.

This afternoon, Judy Maysles, David's wife, dropped "goodies" off on the back porch entrance. Ham and other food. The Beales were aggravated, as they though Judy had been spying on them, under the upstairs porch while they conversed. I had been in town at the time.

Thursday, 24 July, 1975

It was too hot; I was busy. I had to take the radio that Jackie gave Big Edie to Amagansett to have three batteries placed in it because we didn't know how nor what kind of batteries. Later, David Maysles phoned and Peter Beard phoned. Peter is to arrive tomorrow to see Edie. Big Edie is very nervous.

Friday, August 1, 1975

Little Edie was in a bathing suit, so I put my black one on. Awful heat! This record-breaking weather will be remembered for a long time. David Maysles arrived, looking hot and tired. Later, on the upstairs porch with Big Edie, David gave me $50 for the sign he had asked for.

Saturday, August 2, 1975

This terrible heat wave continues, so I decided to sleep downstairs tonight in the kitchen-studio. Little Edie even suggested it. It was quite easy to move stretcher and the newspapers. I remained all night in the kitchen. The black rat didn't bother me.

This afternoon, Big Edie gave me a small check to buy another bathing suit at Brill's Store on North Main St. A cooler one. I returned with a bathing suit that looks like silk and is black and white. Big Edie liked it.

Monday, August 4, 1975

The fleas are really too difficult! I had to fix my instep and ankles with drug store items and meditate. Later, I drove to the village and back. I bought liver for Big Edie at the I.G.A. They will cook it on the hot plate somehow.

I spent the night in my room. *Never* again will I even think of spending the night in the kitchen no matter how hot the Eye Room is.

I turned on my electric fan this evening. I hadn't used it before, as I thought it would just blow dust, dirt, and old hot air around. However, it did help.

Tuesday, August 5, 1975

I didn't put my new bathing suit on because of the fleas. Little Edie had hers on today. The Maysles arrived early with their camera equipment. Big Edie made gin drinks for them, but didn't have one. David and Al worked outside by the house near the windows.

Wednesday, August 6, 1975

The flea situation is worse and requires constant attention. Terrible! The hedge fleas and cat fleas may drive me out of Grey Gardens. I feel almost powerless against them. This afternoon, I drove into town with the damn fleas following me.

Friday, August 8, 1975

Little Edie came downstairs this morning to tell me that a Mr. Hunt, owner of The National Enquirer had been on the phone from Florida. Little Edie granted him an interview on Wednesday.

A woman asked me to read palms tonight at a party in East Hampton, so I accepted.

Tuesday, August 12, 1975

Big Edie received a warm, friendly note from Jacqueline, who is in New York City now.

I found my scissors and trimmed my long grey-silver hair and cut my bangs.

Wednesday, August 13, 1975

We certainly expected a visit from Mr. Hunt of The National Enquirer, but there was nothing... not even a telephone call. Just as well. I went out early as I had to get Big Edie one lamb chop, and then on to Brill's for a dress for Little Edie that her Mother had selected over the phone.

I wanted to sit outside, but the fleas and flies bothered me. Also, there's a strong, unpleasant smell. The cesspool under the upstairs porch has overflowed. A pool has formed on the ground now that I wouldn't want to wander near. However, I noticed the raccoons walked around the edge.

Late this afternoon, Mr. Hunt called after all. He has arrived from Florida with a photographer. Big Edie didn't care to see them this evening.

Thursday, August 14, 1975

David Maysles phoned and seemed excited. The Beale movie will open at Lincoln Center in New York City. They want Little Edie to attend.

The National Enquirer people arrived around 2:00 PM. Big Edie asked me to be here, but I remained out of the way. They went into the kitchen-studio with Little Edie.

Friday, August 15, 1975

It's hot! The cats are ill with distemper. One sick cat lies on Big Edie's bed all the time. But, by the magic of Grey Gardens, one cat dies and another takes its place.

I intend to read palms at another party, this time in Springs. My car is not working, so will be driven there and back. Little Edie will have to wait up for me again. Big Edie said I should dress more like a Gypsy, with big earrings, but I just wore black pants and a black silk jacket from Manila and a blue headband over my forehead. The jacket was about fifty years old that I found in one of my old trunks. I like to be comfortable.

Monday, August 18, 1975

The Maysles have confirmed that the Beale movie will premiere at Lincoln Center about September 27th. The film will be named "Grey Gardens".

I was cold on my stretcher last night, because of a change in the weather. I woke up about 3:00 AM from the cold, but I didn't want to get up for a blanket, as I didn't want the fleas jumping around. I decided to remain chilly.

Little Edie is doing a lot of jumping and stamping around the upstairs hall, as she is most excited about the movie now. She will dash over to me, give my hair a yank, shout something-or-other and rush off. Big Edie trying to keep her calm by using her wit and ordering her concerning the running of the house. The real Grey Gardens must remain as if nothing is happening in New York City. I wonder if it's possible…

Thursday, August 28, 1975

After breakfast, I walked outside, a really beautiful day. Looking up at the sky, I noticed a black and white kite flying over the top of the roof. It had a wire string attached to it that went way out of sight. The huge kite just remained in its position, never seen anything like it! I decided to report this to Big Edie. She called the local Police Department immediately. We were worried about it being a listening device, or even a bomb. Little Edie was busy with the cats at the time. Within minutes, a patrol car drove in and an officer got out and stared at the thing.

"Miss Wright… That's just a kite."

"Perhaps it is, Officer, and perhaps it's not. Mrs. Beale is quite concerned. It shouldn't be hovering over her house like that! It seems like an invasion of privacy."

We both stared a long time at it. The officer mumbled, "It's just a kite."

"Perhaps. I don't like it there."

"I'll see what I can do. It sure has a long wire."

The police officer drove off with his lights flashing. I went upstairs to tell Big Edie.

By the time I had finished talking with the Beales about it, the kite or whatever had disappeared. Little Edie was angry. She hadn't known about it until then.

"Well… I certainly missed the fun… and I *never* have any! Why didn't you tell me, Mother! I never have any fun in this place. God!"

SEPTEMBER 1975

Monday, September 1, 1975

I bought *The National Enquirer* for the Beales. There is nothing in it about the interview here. There was a small item about Jack Bouvier's grave at The Most Holy Trinity cemetery. They thought the Bouvier plot appeared neglected, and had a photograph of it in the paper.

Wednesday, September 3, 1975

This afternoon, Little Edie came into my room to tell me, "It's in the *Daily News* today, Lois, about the Manheims!" She had the paper in her hand. "Our next door neighbor, Paul E. Manheim... you know he's a millionaire, had a burglary in his New York City apartment!" Edie looked pleased. "Just think... $750,000 stolen last night, while he was away... mostly jade art. Don't you love jade?"

"Yes, I do."

"I think the Manheims may have caused our raid... you just can't tell... but I'll find out someday. The *Beale* Office will keep right on investigating. Lois, you *never* know when a burglary will take place! Our doors must always be locked! I'm glad that you do guard the downstairs... not too well, but better than nothing. Do you think the officials in East Hampton will try to blame us for the theft?"

"No... we haven't left the Hamptons in years. Your Mother knows that. I haven't been to New York City since 1963. I didn't do it."

"Oh, I know *you* didn't, but they still might try to implicate us, living next door to his summer home. Mr. Manheim should have been guarding his collection, but he was down here."

"I guess it's all insured."

Little Edie appeared disappointed. "Rich people are terrible! I hope it was a total loss! All they do is drink, take drugs, and have sex every minute. What I could tell you about the Rich! No responsibility! Except for the 'self-made' ones, like Cap."

Edie closed the door on her way out, leaving a few more fleas in my room.

Saturday, September 6, 1975

Today was busy! At 5:30 PM, Big Edie's son, Bouvier, and his son, and a girl he is engaged to, arrived as expected. We all sat talking in the upstairs hall. Just after they left, David Maysles arrived unexpectedly. He had loads of news about the movie. An ad for it will be in *The Sunday Times*. He said Bouvier Beale knew. The Beales disagreed with that. David also mentioned that Jacqueline Onassis and Lee Radziwill just recently found out. Apparently, Jackie felt all right about *Grey Gardens*, but Lee was a little angry. Big Edie looked stunning this evening, and so did Little Edie. I wore my white tennis jacket, as Big Edie had asked me to. David said he would show the film at Grey Gardens soon. We can hardly wait!

Sunday, September 7, 1975

There is a full page ad in *The Times* all about the movies that will be released at The Lincoln Center Film Festival. David stopped by again.

Monday, September 8, 1975

Little Edie was talking about the meetings between John Davis and David Maysles. She is upset and worried about them. Davis wrote *The Bouviers, an American Family.* He is Big Edie's sister's son.

Tuesday, September 9, 1975

Early this morning, the Beales found one of their favorite cats, Hippy, dead. She was about fourteen years old.

Little Edie worked hard to defrost the old refrigerator, but she couldn't do it. However, she did clean it.

The kitchen stove oven has stopped working. I can't light it; I guess the gas is getting low.

Thursday, September 11, 1975

I don't know what the Beales did with Hippy's body.

Monday, September 15, 1975

The fleas are gone! We are all extremely happy about the matter. It seems unbelievable. Every living thing here feels like a battle has been won! Oh, joy!

It was cold last night. I got up at 7:00 AM and turned the heat on for Big Edie.

The Beales and I talked about the film release in New York City. A difficult problem for Little Edie to go in. I certainly can't take care of Grey Gardens alone! Brooks will have to remain inside day and night. He spent most of the summer cutting the grass and mopping the floors. Big Edie said she would not stay alone with just Brooks, so I can't go in to N.Y.C.

Little Edie will have to have something new to wear.

After dinner, I told Big Edie I wanted to hear Mystery Theater on my radio. She commented, "I don't understand why you want to hear that when there is so much mystery here!"

Thursday, September 18, 1975

Tonight, I heard that Patricia Hearst had been found in California. We had been worrying about her for such a long time! Big Edie had prayed for her every night since she was kidnapped. Thought she was wonderful to have survived. Now, if only Patty could be taken home to rest and recover from her ordeal. Big Edie had a newspaper photo of her on the wall.

A reporter from *The National Star* weekly paper phoned today and talked a long time to Little Edie. An interview. She said that she is a friend of David Maysles.

Sunday, September 21, 1975

PREMIERE OF *GREY GARDENS* AT GREY GARDENS

We are to have a private showing of the Maysles movie in the early afternoon. A very cloudy day with much fog. Only the Maysles brothers will be here. The Beales asked David if Brooks Hires could also watch, as he is in the movie. David said, "Yes, but no one else." I asked if Jack Helmuth could drive over and see it. He is also in the film, in the birthday scene. Jack had been a friend of the Beales for about fifty years, and a good friend of mine. David and Al said no. Only the ones connected with the house could view it. You would think top secret documents were being shown by the CIA! I talked with Jack on the telephone about it, and he said, "I don't want to watch it; I don't care to be there!"

The Maysles seemed nervous. The Beales were busy getting dressed and putting makeup on for the occasion. I couldn't go out at all, as Little Edie didn't want to unlock a door to let me back in. "A spy might try to gain entrance when the door was opened" or something might happen to me in town, could be kidnapped for information.

David and Al couldn't get the movie machine going. We all waited. About 5:00 PM, Al left and later returned with a professional projectionist. An exhausting day!

The movie was to be viewed on a small screen in the upstairs hall. Little Edie carried only a few old chairs in to the hall, and I brought my only chair out of the Eye Room.

After a while, the equipment started to run correctly and we all sat down. David had brought his recorder with the long mic, and placed heavy earphones on his head. He then asked the Beales for their permission to do an interview before the "Upstairs Hall Premiere" started, and another interview afterward for their reaction.

The projectionist had worked hard and was ready, the Maysles seemed tense, Big and Little Edie were relaxed now and enjoying it. Of course, the Beales gave an excellent interview. It was formal.

At last, the movie started.

"Wow! Wow!" Little Edie kept shouting, until Big Edie said, "I can't hear a word if you keep that up. Stop it, Edie!"

Little Edie subsided. She thought there should be more of her dancing and singing in the film. I was shocked at my image on the screen, as I didn't think I appeared so odd and foreign-looking! It gave me a nervous chill. Al informed me that is "just the way you look." Brooks laughed at the scenes where he was cutting the grass. Big Edie thought the entire movie delightful. The Beales complimented the movie generously on their next interview with David. We all enjoyed it. I went downstairs for a cup of coffee. The Maysles brothers seemed relieved, and shortly departed.

Little Edie said that "Europe will appreciate the Grey Gardens movie better than the Americans. When the money starts rolling in, I'm going to France to live!"

Big Edie told her, "The cats need their dinner now."

Monday, September 22, 1975

This morning, the door from the kitchen-studio into the refrigerator room fell completely off the hinges onto the floor. An unfortunate situation, as the raccoons can now rush into the kitchen at any time they care to. Also, it's much too drafty. It will be a few days before Brooks will be here to nail it back up.

Little Edie said she is going to the movie opening on September 27th. Brooks has been informed and will stay here.

Thursday, September 25, 1975

We had damp weather. I had post office activity this afternoon. A letter had to be mailed Special Delivery, certified to Jacqueline from Big Edie.

Also, I had to cash a Maysles Films check for $80 that they had sent to obtain a C.O.D. package for the Beales. It contained a long, bright red dress, with a red shawl to cover a person's head. It had been ordered from some store, out of a newspaper ad, by Big Edie. The dress fit Little Edie, and she seemed pleased. Here Mother had asked the Maysles to pay for it, as Little Edie required something to wear for the opening.

Friday, September 26, 1975

13TH FILM FESTIVAL OPENS AT LINCOLN CENTER

Big Edie said that David had phoned to ask about the dress, and he mentioned that I had been given art credits at the end of the film.

There was a rainstorm tonight. Little Edie tried the red dress on again and decided to wear the head shawl around her hips. Then, she found a scarf for her head.

I gave Edie a man's black cummerbund and a pin like a medal that I had found in the Ladies Village Improvement Society's Bargain Box on Main St. as a "Go to New York City and be a Celebrity" gift. Edie will leave tomorrow, hard to believe!

Saturday, September 27, 1975

PREMIERE OF *GREY GARDENS* IN N.Y.C.

The pouring rain continued, and everyone here was up early. Brooks arrived, and Little Edie asked him to leave! She said that she is *not* going to attend the film opening. "The tracks on the Long Island Rail-Road are too wet!" Brooks left.

David Maysles telephoned from his office in N.Y.C. and was quite upset about Edie's attitude. It's in today's *Daily News* that Edie Bouvier Beale will attend.

The Maysles arranged for a car and driver to arrive at Grey Gardens around 5:30 PM to drive Little Edie into Lincoln Center. Edie changed her mind about going, and left wearing the long red dress with the shawl around her hips.

Brooks returned in time to cook Big Edie's dinner on the bedroom hot plate. I just cannot cook in there with all the cats roaming all over the tables, chair, beds, and, of course, the floor.

Brooks spent the night in the upstairs hall. He had brought an old mattress with him from his little house. Brooks slept in his work clothes. Quiet here.

Sunday, September 28, 1975

While I was out getting the *Sunday Times* and the *Daily News*, a police car arrived at Grey Gardens, and Brooks talked with the officer. Little Edie had sent the police. It seemed that a cat had knocked the telephone off the hook in Big Edie's room yesterday evening, and that's why the phone never rang once last night.

After the officer left, Big Edie talked with her daughter in N.Y.C. "The movie is a great success!" she said. She is going to see it again tonight.

Monday, September 29, 1975

We didn't hear from Edie all day! We even had the phones checked, and all are working. Brooks is taking care of the cats and raccoons and Big Edie. I went for the papers, but didn't stay out long as Big Edie was nervous. At last, the Maysles telephoned. They hadn't heard from Little Edie. She was staying at The Martha Washington Hotel, but checked out at noon. Odd? We decided she would be on a certain evening train from Penn. Station. I drove off to the meet the train at the East Hampton rail-road station, but there was no Edie and no train, so I cut the motor, turned the car lights off, and waited.

Shortly, a police car drove up, red lights flashing. An officer told me to return to Grey Gardens because Edie Beale was home. Big Edie had phoned the police to tell me, as she thought I would sit there forever. I had missed the train, and Little Edie had taken a cab. Our celebrity had returned.

I started the Ghia's engine and returned to the house to find Little Edie sitting in her mother's room, starting on a dinner that Brooks had cooked. He had opened the rear door for me, and then we went upstairs. Brooks had on a small flowered apron over his usual tan workpants to indicate that he was the hotplate chef and had been doing all the Beale cooking. Little Edie was eating and talking and laughing. "Hello, Lois, sorry about the station, but you know how I like to take cabs! That's why I didn't call, and I was looking in shop windows this afternoon before the train left Penn. Station."

"Did you enjoy the opening?"

"Oh, yes. I had a standing ovation at Lincoln Center! Listen, kiddo… I'm going on with my *career* now. Nothing can stop me, not even my rotten relatives… Get it! But Mother is the star of *Grey Gardens*. There was a long line of people… fans… interviewers… wanting to speak with Mother. They were at the party after the opening. You, you dummy, Lois! You left the telephone of the hook, I could have been murdered! You did it on purpose… so you wouldn't be bothered!"

"I did *not*! A cat must have knocked the receiver off."

"Well… You should have checked… See how I watch everything, but I can't expect anyone else to be as efficient as I am. It's the way my father brought me up! All you can do is paint. You needed very *strict* Catholic training… but *you* didn't have it, that's why you didn't notice the telephone. God!"

"Stop talking that way to Lois. Where are your manners, out in the Italian garden? I think one of your cats—that I had to take care of—moved the receiver. She shouldn't have been in here. Anyway, she probably wanted a vacation from *you* and all the commotion… You better take those good clothes off now, you might need them again, Edie… and get me a chocolate milk."

"All right, Mother. What do you want me to do first?"

"Don't just stand there! Get me the milk first!"

Brooks asked me to let him out, and that he would return tomorrow for his check. He untied the pink and white apron to leave it for Little Edie. She snatched it out of his hands. "Thank you, Brooks. There is something important we need you for tomorrow, come early."

Brooks and I left the bedroom, and the stars went back to their usual lifestyle.

Tuesday, September 30, 1975

Big Edie received a note from Nancy Tuckerman. She wrote that Jackie had to leave for London, and that she had just left and didn't know about the film showing at Lincoln Center Saturday.

In the *Daily News*, there is an attractive photograph of Little Edie and a write-up about the film.

The floor right in front of Big Edie's bedroom upstairs was in terrible condition from all the rain recently. It was dangerous; anyone could have fallen through to the living room. It is long drop! Brooks repaired it as best he could.

OCTOBER & NOVEMBER 1975

Friday, October 3, 1975

This morning in the kitchen-studio, I gave Little Edie "the Friday Five," as we call it. Her mother never knew, but every Friday, Little Edie collected a five-dollar bill from me. It is all I can do to help out now.

Saturday, October 4, 1975

I drove into town and back. David Maysles's car was here when I returned. We all chatted in Big Edie's room. We are glad the floor is fixed! David said that *Newsweek* and *Time* magazines will mention *Grey Gardens*. He gave Big Edie a gift for her birthday, which is tomorrow.

Sunday, October 5, 1975

MRS. EDITH BOUVIER BEALE'S BIRTHDAY

Today, Big Edie is 80 years old. Coincidentally, two Englishmen from *Harper's Bazaar* in London had made plans to interview Big and Little Edie today. They had seen the movie at Lincoln Center. All morning, the Beales were busy getting ready. Big Edie is an expert at applying lipstick and black eyebrow coloring. It brought out the lovely blue of her eyes, and the dark brows gave her an interesting dramatic appearance. Little Edie might forget her lipstick, if Big Edie and I didn't remind her. By 2:00 PM, when the *Harper's Bazaar* people were expected, the Beales were in the upstairs hall. Little Edie had on the long red dress. Her mother asked me to remain in the hall.

The photographer and writer from the magazine arrived late. They had a long talk with the Beales, and many pictures were taken of the Beales together. Little Edie told them she wouldn't pose with anyone except her mother! The photographer took a couple of shots of my tall, thin mural on heavy paper that stated, "Hail Big Edie." It was hung on the hall wall.

Little Edie brought her old record playing machine out and put a record on. She wanted to dance to some Spanish music, and, for a short time, she did. It looked more like a scene in Spain or Italy than East Hampton.

Later, the polite writer and photographer left. They were returning to England tonight. Big Edie granted the interview, as she thought the men sounded older on the phone, and she wanted to see an older man for a change, someone she could be interested in.

Not too long after the young *Harper's Bazaar* people departed, Big Edie's son Bouvier and her grandson Ridgely and his fiancée arrived for a small birthday party in the hall. Little Edie served ice cream and cake and the guests brought a bottle of wine with them. We all had a pleasant time. The raccoons watched us from outside the windows; a melted container of ice cream was placed on the ledge for them. The cats, except for a few important favorites, remained locked in Big Edie's bedroom. She never wanted Bouvier to know how many really roamed around Grey Gardens.

Monday, October 6, 1975

Today, I had my first recorded interview as a Palmist and Mystic. It took place at an office on The Circle in East

Hampton and had nothing to do with the Beales or their movie. I never mentioned where I lived or that I even knew the Beales, as Little Edie asked me not to. I had to always exist as "the Ghost of Grey Gardens." The magazine is called *Fascinación* and published in Venezuela. I talked quite a while, and then analyzed the interviewer's hands, while a photographer, Anthony Hitchcock, took photos. A couple of months earlier, *Fascinación* did a write-up on Little Edie and Peter Maicas photographed her many times and also the house. Big Edie wouldn't meet them, much to their disappointment.

On my way home, I stopped at the stationery story and picked up *The National Star*. There is an article in it about the Beales.

All the electricity off upstairs, wire trouble again. Big Edie was on the phone trying to get someone to fix it. Will go to bed by candlelight, not difficult for me, but, of course, the Beales can't cook on the hotplate.

I was standing in their room when Little Edie said, "I think it's just awful that my spoiled, terrible, kid brother refuses to see his own Mother's movie! He refused to see it! What do you think of a rat like that?"

"Edie! Stop talking! I'm trying to get an electrician, not analyze Buddy! It's imperative that I get an electrician! Do you want the house to catch fire? Lois, hand her a fiddle so she can play while Rome burns."

Little Edie and I laughed, while Big Edie went back to dialing numbers. We knew she wouldn't allow anything to ever happen to Grey Gardens.

Later, I lit candles in my room, and Big Edie directed her daughter to bring out the Sterno.

Wednesday, October 8, 1975

I obtained both *Time* and *Newsweek* magazines. There is wonderful write-up in *Newsweek* about the film. There's a photograph of Little Edie at Lincoln Center in *Time*.

David Maysles telephoned from New York and said to buy this week's *Village Voice*, which has a great full-page story about movie.

Thursday, October 9, 1975

An electrician is expected this afternoon. Big Edie asked me not to go out until after he had left. She thought Little Edie might have to go down into the basement with Mr. Stewart and that would leave her alone in the house, and something might happen to them in the basement. In the cellar, they were "out of touch," no communications. I agreed. Not only that, but a burglar could rush in the back door.

By evening, all the electricity was working again. Big Edie paid the bill from her small sum of money.

Friday, October 10, 1975

After dinner last night, a man with the French Broadcasting Co. phoned the Beales for an interview. Little Edie was tired, but said she "might do it sometime." She didn't feel like talking with him.

This afternoon, I brought in ice cream, and chopped meat for all.

Saturday, October 11, 1975

We feel the need here for additional funds, so this evening I composed a letter to send out to all the good restaurants to see if any of them would like a palmist. Years ago, I had read hands at the Sea Spray Inn in East Hampton when Mr. Bailey owned it. The Beales read my letter and liked it much. I made about eight copies to mail.

Monday, October 13, 1975

COLUMBUS DAY

I did all the grocery shopping for Grey Gardens this morning, as we didn't realize it's Columbus Day, and The Newtown wouldn't deliver on a holiday. There is never any cat food cans in reserve. It has to come in every day, along with the bread for the numerous raccoons.

I was startled to see tacked on Big Edie's bedroom wall, two or three signs cut from a newspaper magazine. They were about a foot high, a foot wide, and in color. Red lettering on white that stated "Free Food." When I asked about them, Little Edie smiled and told me that her mother wanted them in view to remind her that "I'm living here for nothing, isn't that cute!"

"Yes, I'm impressed with the idea, makes me feel like getting free food from somewhere. Certainly would be wonderful…"

"You know, Lois, there is such a thing as food stamps; we have been reading about it. Do you think you could get information without using our names? We wouldn't want the Village Board or the Health Dept. to know about our interest. Just think of the money we could save! You could use the stamps at the I.G.A."

Big and Little Edie looked serious.

"I'll find out what I can do. I think you have to write to the County Center in Riverhead."

"All right, Lois, but be careful! And we want to read the letter before you send it!'

Within a couple of days, I discovered that I would have to contact a Ms. Wheat in the Social Services at Riverhead.

We couldn't help but be amused about the name, Ms. Wheat and food stamps. I wrote her a letter, and then read it to the Beales. Big Edie liked it; however, she thought it too long. "It's one of the best letters I've ever read, Lois, but you don't have to tell them your life's history! Just write a note."

"God!" Little Edie commented. "Don't write it at all! Don't get involved with the government; we could have another raid!"

"Oh, shut up, Edie, I'm thinking of the cats. Here, kitty, have some of my bacon."

I wrote a note, it was approved by the Beales, and I mailed it. Of course, their name was not mentioned. Since I bought all my own food, I could request assistance. I did have to state my address. Eventually, Big Edie signed a paper to prove that I live there. The Suffolk County Dept. of Social Services entered my life for the first time, and proceeded to be a great help. No one else knew, and the "Free Food" signs remained in place.

Wednesday, October 15th, 1975

Brooks phoned. I had a good breakfast. I still have to wear a hat in the refrigerator room, as a raccoon or rat could land on your head from the ceiling where the open spaces are. Brooks only repaired side wall openings.

Little Edie wants to see *Nashville*. It's playing at the local theater. She hasn't been anywhere since she attended her own movie in New York City. I don't know if she will go or not.

A raccoon killed something in the old house tonight and it made a terrible sound. I hope it was only a rat. To hear it all on a soundtrack, one would think one was living in darkest Africa.

This afternoon, I met an acquaintance in the village and received a shock. She introduced me to Doris Francisco.

During the course of conversation, I was amazed to learn that she knew the Beales, had been having long conversations on the phone with them. She seemed equally astonished to discover that I am the only one living at Grey Gardens. Doris Francisco is most unusual. I don't care to make comparisons, but it's necessary to describe her. She appears to look like a cross between Lauren Bacall and Melina Mercouri, with a voice reminiscent of Tallulah Bankhead. Really! I returned home and told the Beales. They let me know the truth. Doris Francisco *is* the mysterious caller. I wondered why it was kept a secret. Perhaps I would have found out some day?

Doris had never been to Grey Gardens, nor had she ever met Big Edie, Little Edie, or me in person, as she had been living in Connecticut. One of Little Edie's young nephews had a store in Westport, Connecticut, selling waterbeds, and Doris had met him there. He mentioned Big Edie and suggested she call Mrs. Beale when she moved to East Hampton. Doris phoned the Beales and talked, but they wouldn't let her visit.

I suggested to Beales that they open the door for Doris to come in.

Saturday, October 18, 1975

Today we had another rain storm with heavy dark clouds and strong winds. Little Edie decided to see *Nashville* today, and her mother gave her movie ticket and cab money. I couldn't drive Edie there, as Big Edie wouldn't "stay alone a minute!" At 1:45 PM, I locked Little Edie out the front door, and she left in Schaefer's Taxi. My instructions were to remain upstairs until Edie called to be let back inside. Couldn't even go downstairs for a cup of coffee, so I looked forward to the return of Miss Beale. Big Edie and I waited a long time. About 5:30, we conferred about telling the police

of Little Edie's disappearance. The cats were getting
alarmed, too! At 6:00 PM, we heard pounding on the door,
and I raced down to unlock all the many locks and bolts and
flung the large door wide open. It was Edie, and she looked
marvelous, but dripping wet. She slipped quickly inside, and
we soon had the door tightly secured once again.

Big Edie's voice drifted towards us. "Edie! Edie! Oh,
Edie… come right up! Where have you been? We were
going to phone the police!"

"I'm coming, Mother! It was a three-hour movie."

We ran up to the bedroom.

"I had to walk home in the rain. God! Did I get wet!
That stupid cab driver wasn't waiting for me out in front of
the theater."

"Why not?" I asked.

"Because I went into the powder room after the movie to
look in those big, clear mirrors they have, and I missed the
cab. The idiot didn't have to drive off right away! East
Hampton! You can have it! I'm going to Nashville!"

Little Edie started to dance around the small room and
shout some lines from one of the songs she had heard.

"Edie! Stop that stamping… the floor could give way!
Stop it… the cats haven't been fed. Oh… go on and go to
Nashville. Go on… I don't care!"

Little Edie stopped. "Lois has to see the picture
tomorrow. I want her to see it!"

"All right, I'll go tomorrow."

"I want your opinion of Altman."

Sunday, October 19, 1975

I drove to the theater to see *Nashville*. I enjoyed it and
drove home. Edie wants to see it again. I doubt if she will…
and I hope not.

Thursday, October 23, 1975

After breakfast, Big Edie called me into her room to tell me that she heard on the radio that Caroline Kennedy was nearly killed in a bombing! She is safe, not hurt, but one man killed. It happened in London. Little Edie decided not to go to Nashville, as someone might try to kill her! Better to stay here and not get murdered, if possible. The Beales wondered if they should phone Jacqueline and offer advice. "Poor Jackie," Little Edie said.

Friday, October 31, 1975

HALLOWEEN

A quiet Halloween night here, no one came near. Nothing special going on… I did find without looking my lost scissors. They have been lost for the past week, and I missed them. However, I put my left hand on them, while sitting at the card table in the Eye Room. Big Edie said Tom Logan "brought them back." I didn't even notice that they were there!

Saturday, November 1, 1975

David Maysles phoned. He informed Little Edie about a long write-up regarding *Grey Gardens* in the November issue of *Vogue* magazine. David read it to her, and Little Edie started shouting at the top of her lungs, as she didn't care for the article by Charlotte Curtis. She wrote that the movie is "a shocker!" David said he would arrive here tomorrow. He just returned from California, where he attended a private film showing of *Grey Gardens*. Edie banged the receiver down.

This evening, David and Judy Maysles arrived about 5:00. They brought *Vogue* with them. A great deal of loud and outraged indignation by the Beales.

Judy said, "I'm going to have a baby next month!"

Little Edie answered, "I know that... David... If she dies in childbirth, don't feel badly... I'll marry you!"

During the silence, Little Edie stared at them and smiled. A short time later, the Maysles were locked out.

Tuesday, November 4, 1975

I remained home while Little Edie left to vote at Guild Hall in East Hampton. A Democratic worker had telephoned, and then arranged for someone to drive Edie in to the village and back. I asked Little Edie to vote Yes on the E.R.A. for me. She said she would.

The Beales are still angry about Charlotte Curtis and her awful write-up.

Wednesday, November 5, 1975

This morning, before 10:00, the phone rang and Big Edie answered it. A pleasant-sounding woman wanted to speak to me. She asked if I knew of an astrologer she could consult. I didn't know of one.

An hour later, a call came in for Mrs. Beale from Florida. Something to do with *The National Enquirer*. They wanted information about Bouvier Beale. Big Edie didn't tell them anything.

Friday, November 7, 1975

LITTLE EDIE'S BIRTHDAY

I had to shop for Big Edie yesterday, going here and there, getting this and that for the party. When I returned, *The London Times* was on the wire from England. They told Miss Edith Bouvier Beale that *Grey Gardens* was a brilliant, stunning film. Little Edie asked if the Queen had seen it. They didn't know.

After the conversation, Little Edie left for The Most Holy Trinity church in a taxi. She wanted to take Communion. She was gone two hours. She wanted to be ready for her birthday.

This morning, Big Edie and I wished her a Happy Birthday, and, of course, her mother, The Great Singer, sang, "Happy Birthday to you, Happy Birthday, dear Edie, Happy Birthday to you!" Big Edie had a beautiful, trained voice and we enjoyed hearing her sing. She was very talented, and not appreciated enough. She certainly was not at all appreciated by the public, who never had the chance to appreciate her. Because she married, the public never knew of her wonderful ability. Very sad.

She then told her daughter of the horrors of having a baby, as if Little Edie didn't know by now. Big Edie soon became the center of our attention for having gone through so much, and we felt pleased that we had managed to arrive on this earth, and Big Edie talked about her mother with fond memory.

After lunch, I drove into town for four pints of ice cream. The small cake had been delivered yesterday.

I gave Little Edie her gifts, and she had presents from the Maysles. About 3:00 PM, Big Edie phoned her son Buddy in Bridgehampton. He wasn't home, but his son Ridgely was there with Carla, his bride-to-be, and her brother, Jim. They would drive over. Big Edie asked me to wear my white tennis jacket again.

"My rotten brother," Little Edie said. "He's too *mad* to come because I made a *movie*. God! He hasn't seen it, but he's *mad*... American men! That's what happens when they get married... the wife rules, and they don't want their sister-in-law making a decent movie. They want to be everything... I think it's sad..."

Ridgely, Carla, and Jim arrived at 4:30, and we all sat in the upstairs hall. It was a delightful party, and Big Edie even drank a tiny bit of gin. Wine was also served by Ridgely. Big Edie gave Ridgely and Carla a gold wedding ring I had, and Carla was delighted.

I had given Little Edie a red silk shirt, made in Spain, that I had bought in the Bargain Box for 75¢. It was stunning and looked new, folded in tissue paper and placed in an old Mark, Fore & Strike box. Little Edie had the red shirt arranged on her head when the guests arrived today it looked most becoming!

Saturday, November 8, 1975

PALM READING AT GREY GARDENS

Since the better restaurants in East Hampton didn't respond to the letters I sent out, it was decided that I should do hand analysis here… in the kitchen-studio. Big Edie would make the appointments when the clients phoned. I called a few key people to let them know where I would be.

Little Edie strongly suggested that I watch them every minute and under no circumstances should they be allowed into any other part of the house, and to enter by the back door. The Beales would stay locked in their bedroom until I had finished.

A woman and a man arrived to have their palms read this afternoon. They were quite interested in the reading. I only charged five dollars per person, so I earned ten dollars. However, I gave Little Edie two dollars. She would expect her profit as soon as I had locked the people out.

"Lois, did they pay you?"

"Oh, yes, Edie. Here's your money."

Little Edie would take it quickly, and place the one dollar bills in one of Mr. Onassis's leather vest-coat pockets, smiling pleasantly, and then walk over to the kitchen-studio mirror to study her reflection for a while. I went up to Big Edie's room to tell her about my success and she would nod her head with pleasure and ask me if I thought it was a good idea to get some ice cream.

Monday, November 10, 1976

This morning, a large puddle of urine suddenly appeared on the floor in the front section of the Eye Room, the part with all the windows. I heard it pour on the floor, and could smell it. A raccoon in the attic, no doubt. I went over to my stack of newspapers to put over it to absorb the water. I looked up to study the ceiling and found it to be dry and clean, nothing. Odd. Perhaps it was a spirit of some kind… or Tom "Tex" Logan, but why would he do a thing like that? I called Little Edie in about it. She just laughed and said she would check the attic right away. I decided to place my gold cross on. Big Edie couldn't understand how it happened, but didn't think poor Tom was responsible. Perhaps it was the ghost of the sea captain who Edie said had built the house having some fun. He used to stay in my room a great deal before he died.

Mr. Hunt of *The National Enquirer* telephoned. He asked Big Edie to telephone her niece, Jackie, about her daughter Caroline and the bombing. Big Edie agreed to. Mr. Hunt was so insistent! I drove in to town and back. The Beales had phoned Jacqueline at her home and also the Viking Press, but they had just missed her at both places. Big Edie decided not to bother calling again, however, Mr. Hunt continued to phone about it. The Beales were to be in *The National Enquirer* in January, he said. They never used last summer's interview. Today's *National Enquirer* states that Jacqueline Onassis's daughter is in *great* danger of being kidnapped in London. I don't see what Big Edie can do. We have enough trouble trying not to be kidnapped from Grey Gardens.

Wednesday, November 12, 1975

This morning, Big Edie gave me a check to buy a small camera. She used to enjoy taking pictures, and now she wanted me to. Said I am a good photographer. Little Edie didn't like cameras and certainly didn't like snapping pictures. I went into town and returned with a new camera. Little Edie said a strange man appeared on the property while I was gone and she talked to him form the window… a detective or a reporter. She wouldn't let him in.

Later, *The National Enquirer* phoned once again. He knew nothing about the stranger on the grounds. Anyway, *The National Enquirer* interviewer arrived about 5:00 PM, and Little Edie talked with him in the dining room while I conversed with Big Edie about the camera. Little Edie wore the "Lincoln Center" red dress again and looked like celebrity! He asked Little Edie about me, said he met me last August. I guess she told him I died or something. He wants to arrive next week to photograph the $50,000 worth of clothes that a writer from the *Daily News* reported the Beales had received as a gift from Mr. Onassis! The interviewer wanted to take some pictures of Edie wearing some of the clothes, and Edie would have enjoyed that, bus she didn't have $50,000 worth of clothes from Mr. Onassis.

After *The National Enquirer* man had been locked out, Edie asked her mother what she should do.

"Oh, Edie… just go through some trunks in the attic, and perhaps you can find some old clothes to wear from him." We all laughed. It would be quite a project, but it sounded like fun. However, it never happened, as Little Edie simply could not locate any clothes that looked like $50,000 worth. Of course, she didn't have much time to devote to the idea. I offered to lend her all my clothes to help out a big, but it didn't work.

Thursday, November 13, 1975

"The rain started last night, quite a North-Easter, I guess. Rain came down in such torrents, it woke me up. I love to hear it, even if the floors get drenched.

Big Edie talked on the phone with Nancy Tuckerman today. They had a long, pleasant conversation, even mentioned the movie.

Rat problems here, one in Little Edie's closet. She left the door open so it could race out, or hopefully, a few cats would go in after it. No action, until a couple of hours later, when I was just leaving my room, and Little Edie was striding down the upstairs hall, when The Rat suddenly appeared "out of nowhere" and leaped at Little Edie, striking her on the Onassis leather coat-vest. At first, Edie thought it was a cat, as she couldn't see too well.

"Get down! God! It's a rat! Mother! A rat just jumped on me! I'm in the hall! Lois! Get your club!" Edie yelled.

I could hear Big Edie calling from her room as I turned to select a proper weapon. "Edie! Oh, Edie! Come in here! Quickly! Get my male cats after it! Let them out the other door. Hurry up! And get my stick. Where's Lois?"

Little Edie ran to execute her mother's instructions. I couldn't see the rat now. The males roamed slowly into the hall looking disinterested, Little Edie in the middle of them.

"God! They don't care. I'm not going to spend another year in this horrible place. I'm going to marry Governor Carey!"

"Edie!" I shouted. "It's better to have a rat or two around than go through the tortures of having eleven or twelve children like his poor wife had to. Now she's dead!"

"Well... I could go to Florida and have a nightclub act... and hit the beach every day."

"And get murdered!" Big Edie's raised voice could be heard from her room. Somehow, she always heard what we were saying in the hall, even if Little Edie whispered. It was an unusual "gift" she possessed.

Later in the day, an old female cat, a friend of Little Edie's, found The Rat, and, as a favor to Edie, killed it for her.

"That cat has great character," I told Little Edie.

"Yes, Lois... She's a mother cat, had more kittens than the Careys had babies. I think she's tired of it... but the males keep screwing her. I'll have to try and stop tem... Black Cat always on top of her. God!"

The subject was changed, as Big Edie wanted me to drive into town to Brill's to pick up a pair of sneakers that she had ordered for her daughter. The Beales loved sneakers, and when Big Edie had to go in to New York City on the train after Tom, she always wore them.

Sunday, November 16, 1975

At last, Jacqueline returned her aunt's telephone call. She phoned from New Jersey and they all talked quite a while, a pleasant conversation. As usual, the Beales sounded as if they were chatting from a "lovely suite at the Plaza Hotel." Jacqueline talked about the *Grey Gardens* write-up in the November *Vogue*. She seemed fine about the movie, and Big Edie was happy about that.

I was having a cup of coffee in the kitchen-studio when I happened to glance up and noticed a strange man standing outside in back of the screen door. I asked him what he wanted. He was a photographer. "I'm Mr. Howard," he said. "Could I see the Beales?"

"You should telephone first. They never see anyone who just arrives on the back porch. But I'll tell them you are here."

I closed the wooded door, bolted all the locks, and went upstairs to knock at the Beales' bedroom door.

"A photographer wants to see you, Edie! I have the door locked. What do you want to do?"

"Get rid of him. Tell him to call if he wants. Thanks, Lois."

I returned to the eager stranger. He had a large camera bag over his shoulder.

"Yes, can I come in now?"

"No. Go somewhere and telephone."

"Where?"

"There are phones in the village."

The photographer left looking depressed, and I went back to my coffee.

Monday, November 17, 1975

This morning, two male cats killed a rat and left it half dead in the middle of Big Edie's bed! She called Little Edie to sweep it off. "It's a horrid brown rat. Hurry up, Edie! The broom is in the bathroom. No, *this* bathroom. And I better contact Brooks to plug up some holes, right away!"

"All right, Mother. Where did you say the broom is?"

The moon was bright this evening. It must have inspired us, as Little Edie wrote poetry and I was busy painting. A perfect night. The cats were quiet, even the raccoons. Perhaps the raccoons were having a meeting outside, and the cats must have been meditating. Big Edie didn't call for anything.

Wednesday, November 19, 1975

The electric went off upstairs again. I can smell the Sterno this morning.

A photographer from *The National Enquirer* was at the front door early this afternoon. Little Edie asked me to tell him to "go away, that Mother wasn't well." She knew he had arrived to photograph her in some of "the $50,000 worth of clothes Mr. Onassis had sent" and take pictures of all the valuable clothes hanging here and there." *The Daily News* misinformation certainly caused us trouble!

Little Edie was active tonight, as most of the females were in heat, and the electric was still off. Having the lights on would have helped Edie separate the males from the female cats.

I had lit candles in the Eye Room and, as it was starting to get cool, I put a hot-water bottle under the sheet on my stretcher. I went to bed late, as I was reading the Tarot cards. A few years ago, Jacqueline had given Little Edie a beautiful Tarot deck, but she couldn't find them. In 1976, Edie located the gift, and, to my pleasant surprise, gave them to be. Little Edie liked to tell the future without benefit of cards. She believed Cap assisted her.

Friday, November 21, 1975

Early this morning, a beautiful pink kitten died on Big Edie's chest. She had tried for days to keep it alive and the kitten seemed to know it. Later, when I went into her room, Big Edie was sad about it, and the pink kitten's body was still under her chin. Magic, or perhaps Love from Big Edie turned the kitten's body into a lovely clean object that resembled a delightful tiny pink kitten powder puff that stayed on Big Edie's bed. The other cats and kittens paid no attention to it, as they knew it belonged to Big Edie and was something special. About three weeks later, it had disappeared, as if it had turned to pink dust.

The electric was working upstairs, but it was still a cold night in my room.

I read palms at Grey Gardens this afternoon. After the reading drove into town and bought some bacon for the Beales and a candy bar for Little Edie. It was great to feel extravagant.

This evening, Dogcat and Pinky killed another rat. While they were doing that, I move my huge "Silver Cross" painting on Masonite board from the kitchen-studio floor up onto the antique coal stove. Little Edie liked it there and wanted to buy it, but I didn't want to sell the painting. It's my chapel...

We have no plans for Thanksgiving tomorrow. Big Edie said that she "hopes someone sends her turkey." I guess we will just have our usual food under the roof of Grey Gardens, feeling love and safety and no disease.

Thursday, November 27, 1975

THANKSGIVING

Rain all day. Big Edie was upset this morning, as her last kitten from a certain litter was found dead on her bed when she woke up. It was "Pinky Two." By 4:00 PM, it was still reposing on the Onassis blanket, under a couple of Kleenex. Big Edie disliked "The Grim Reaper" and waited as long as possible before giving in to his demands.

I painted in the kitchen-studio, worked on the eyes in a portrait and started another canvas.

The phone rang, and Little Edie answered it. Al Maysles on the line. He said he phoned to thank everyone for all the birthday cards he received yesterday. Al asked about Thanksgiving dinner here.

Little Edie informed him, "Our Thanksgiving turkey is in the clouds, Al darling."

After he understood that we didn't have any, Al talked a while about coming movie profits and then they hung up.

Around 6:00 PM, two well-dressed women arrived on the front porch and knocked on the door.

"Whoever it is, Lois, *don't* let them inside!" Little Edie shouted, and went into her mother's room.

I unbolted all the locks, and opened the heavy door.

Through the screen door, I found out that they had brought the Beales a magnificent turkey dinner with all the trimmings. It was placed in a wicker basket. I opened the screen door. "I'm Mrs. Tobin," one woman said. "And I live nearby, on West End Road."

I accepted the basket and, after thanking them and locking the doors again, I started up the stairs. The Beales were delighted. "I must write Mrs. Tobin a note," Big Edie commented.

It seemed like the turkey *had* been send down from the sky. "Never lose faith," Big Edie said and smiled.

Little Edie got the knives out. They could balance perfectly a few peas on the tip of a long knife and often did, as they ate their dinner. It amazed me, and I often thought of them as "The Bouvier Sword Swallowers." The Beales didn't really need to use forks, a long kitchen knife would do, even for ice cream, if Little Edie couldn't' find the spoons. I think they liked to keep in practice… in private.

Friday, November 28, 1975

I had to get Little Edie's eye glasses tightened at Dr. York's office on Main Street this morning.

Pinky Two is still on Big Edie's bed under the Kleenex.

"It's all right, Lois, the kitten is dried up from the heat in the room."

"Oh," I said. "I'm sorry it died yesterday."

Little Edie was sitting on the bed opposite her mother's bed looking sadly at the small lump under the white Kleenex. "Poor Pinky Two."

Tonight, Little Edie gave me some additional film write-ups to read, new ones that the Maysles had sent. They were rather shocking… but interesting.

December 1975

Monday, December 1, 1975

Cool and damp. I returned from the village with a letter for the Beales from the Maysles Film, Inc. in New York City. David or Al had enclosed an art-copy paper for me of *Grey Gardens* that will be on the movie posters. In a letter to Big Edie, the Maysles wrote that I helped to inspire the design. An angel within the 'G' of "Grey Gardens." Of course, I was pleased, as I do admire angels and had painted tall, slender ones in blue and silver on thick paper that Little Edie had hung in the room she identifies as her brother's room in the film. She is seen looking at them.

Later on, they changed their mind and used a photograph of Little Edie standing outside in front of Grey Gardens. Perhaps someone decided the Beales lived here and not angels. Well, I can understand that. But it was a lovely, mysterious design someone had put together.

Tuesday, December 2, 1975

Brooks arrived about 1:00 PM to cut the grass! Sometimes it's difficult to know what season it is.

Wednesday, December 3, 1975

Now that the Beales are open about who they talk to when Doris Francisco calls, I knew with whom Little Edie was talking this morning. She answered the phone while Big Edie was moving over from her bed to sit in the rolling chair. We went out to the porch, while Edie and Doris chatted. Usually when Doris calls, she talks with Big Edie, and she usually calls every day.

Some of the cats followed us to the porch room, and some remained in the bedroom as if they wanted to hear the conversation.

A small amount of snow this morning and rather cold. By evening, I could see my breath in the Eye Room. The oil burner was going, the baseboard heaters were warm, but it wasn't adequate. Schenck's oil truck delivered on time, and Jacqueline paid the bills. We always had hot water, however the bath tubs not working, and no showers, so we didn't use too much.

Thursday, December 4, 1975

I wrote a note to the Maysles thanking them for the copy of the *Grey Gardens* design with the "Bouvier Angel." Read it to Big Edie. Brooks arrived and we all went out onto the upstairs porch and snapped some pictures. After that, Brooks repaired the hall ceiling.

At 5:00 PM, I had to stuff newspapers, old envelopes and cardboard in the racks in the windows and around the ledge to keep the cold air from coming in the Eye Room. Quite chilly on the thin canvas stretcher.

Around midnight, Michelle Beale, Big Edie's granddaughter, phoned from Tulsa, Oklahoma. There is a party at Michelle's.

Little Edie refused to wake up and talk, but Big Edie enjoyed the long distance call, "an unusual event." She loved Michelle, as she did all her close relatives, but she admired her granddaughter for being a lawyer in Oklahoma, and very attractive.

Saturday, December 6, 1975

This morning, Big Edie asked me to return the wicker basket that the turkey dinner arrived in on November 27th. She informed me where Mrs. Tobin lived on West End Road and how easy it would be, as they had a circular drive. My brakes were not working again, and I had to rely on the clutch.

"Don't send her, Mother. Lois will *never* find the house!" Little Edie's expression indicated that she expected me to be lost forever.

"I'll make it, and back again," I said.

"She has no sense of direction, Mother!"

"Edie, take Lois on the upstairs porch and point the house out for her. It's only about a block from here!"

"But the Tobins might be home... and I don't want Lois talking with them! She might go inside!"

"Edie! Give this basket to Lois! I want Mrs. Tobin to have it. Do it now!"

"All right. I'll lock her out."

I returned in about three minutes. The Tobins weren't home, but I left the basket there. I don't know why Edie thought I couldn't find the house.

Thursday, December 11, 1975

I couldn't use my car. It will have to go to the garage for repairs. A problem, as Big Edie wants a box mailed to the Maysles. She suggested that I phone Doris Francisco about it. The Beales had been talking to her earlier. I asked for the number. Big and Little Edie never refer to an address book. They memorize all their telephone numbers. I dialed and soon had Doris on the line. Once again, I was startled by her unusually low speaking voice. It wasn't just low or deep, but also it possessed a quality of softness and strength. According to the Beales, Doris had been involved in the theater world in Connecticut, and her mother-in-law owned one of the largest estates in East Hampton near the ocean. Don Francisco, Doris's husband, had died a few years ago, and Doris had never remarried. She had a son, Peter, in boarding school. She was originally from Connecticut, but had summered here for a few years, golf at the Maidstone Club, and all that. But I still didn't know who she was and why she had this contact with the Beales.

Doris said she would drive me into town with the box to mail, and we decided to do this tomorrow.

Two violent male cat fights in the house today. Little Edie threw the upstairs hall table at them. They stopped fighting.

After looking most of the afternoon, I found some Christmas cards I had painted in 1961 of angels. I could use them this year.

Friday, December 12, 1975

About 11:00 AM, Doris Francisco phoned from her home on Duke Drive. She will arrive here at 1:00 PM.

I telephoned the garage on Rail-Road Ave. My car will be ready late this afternoon. New brakes, muffler, heater turned on, and the Ghia checked over. A miracle!

Big Edie didn't feel well, so decided not to meet Doris face-to-face, but Little Edie intended to see Doris downstairs. After she arrived, we chatted in the dining room, and brought Doris into the kitchen-studio to look at my paintings. I had just finished "The Spirit of Edie at the Inlet." A long title, but that is what Edie named it. Doris said she would "like to buy it." Little Edie and I agreed as we were thinking about the car repair bill. I was delighted and Edie understood why I had to sell the painting of her. As a matter of fact, Edie was my art agent, however, she didn't do much about it, except to tell me how much she liked my paintings and collected as many as she could.

I don't recall what Doris had on… a jacket and expensive wool pants. I thought she had the celebrity stamp, and something else… interesting and difficult to define…

Little Edie locked us out, and we soon arrived at the post office where I dispatched the Beale package and collected their mail.

Doris and I enjoyed a milkshake in a soda place under the bridge on North Main Street. It was the first time I'd sat down with anyone in years, outside of Grey Gardens, but it seemed natural. Except for palm reading, I am just as much a recluse as the Beales.

Doris dropped me off at the garage and I drove off in my now-perfect Ghia.

The Maysles sent Big Edie the *London Times Magazine*. A wonderful feature article with colored pictures.

Saturday, December 13, 1975

Little Edie is excited. David Maysles had phoned. He is on his way to London to promote the movie.

I finished another canvas I had been working on, "Cat Spirits."

Brooks expected tomorrow, as Big Edie's bedroom floor needs scraping and mopping and the usual rat-holes blocked.

The Doris Francisco phone calls continue, and once in a while I talk with Doris, too?

After dinner, I started a portrait of the Beales. It's painted on wood and quite large. I liked it so much that I went upstairs to show it to Big and Little Edie. They seemed to like the painting also, except Big Edie wanted her hair longer. I do have a great deal more painting to do on it. Went to "bed" in contentment as always.

Wednesday, December 17, 1975

By evening, I had completed the double portraits and sign-painting. The Beales viewed it upstairs. Little Edie seemed amazed and Big Edie complimented me highly.

"Look, Edie," I said. "Your mother is very *mystical*... and you are protective, almost militant! A *warrior!*"

"I like it!" Big Edie smiled at me.

"Oh, God! Lois... You gave me a double chin!" Little Edie hollered. "But it *is* good! How do you do it, Lois?" Edie spoke the last words slowly and with much thought. Then, "revving up" again, she shouted, "Fix my chin, kiddo, or you're in for trouble!"

"All right, Edie," I shouted back. "I can see it's not right, but I'm not going to touch the scarf!"

"No, the scarf's just perfect. You should design clothes! Don't you want to do that?"

"No, no I don't! Don't say that again or you will be the one in trouble! Design clothes!"

"*Why not?* You could make some money!"

"Edie! I just want to paint and read palms!"

Big Edie looked uncomfortable. "*Stop* that fighting. You want the cats to start? Anyway, the kittens don't like it. Lois, your painting is superb!"

I went back to the kitchen-studio to work on Edie's chin.

Thursday, December 18, 1975

I had to mail a Christmas card to Jacqueline from Big Edie at the post office as it had to be registered. Little Edie didn't have hers ready yet. After I returned, Big Edie gave me a Christmas card that she had selected over the phone from Marley's.

Cold. By 6:00 PM, it was 24 degrees outside, and strong winds. I heard on the radio that it's going into the teens tonight.

David phoned this evening. Said it just happened that he flew back from London with Caroline Kennedy. The trip took five hours, so he had time to talk with her.

Thursday, December 23, 1975

Brooks brought the groceries today from the Newtown instead of the delivery boy. He had some work to do here, so stopped at the store on the way. Along with the regular order, Brooks carried in another large carton packed by the Newtown. Christmas "goodies" from Jacqueline Onassis. Canned ham, candy, cookies, etc. Enclosed was a note from Big Edie's niece. Lee never sent anything, and no one thought about it.

Wednesday, December 24, 1975

CHRISTMAS EVE

There is snow on the ground. My toes were nearly frozen from the cold last night. Gave the Beales my Christmas cards. I took some time on the envelopes, as I always drew the stamp (with a picture of the Beales as if they were on the stamp) and the East Hampton postmark.

Really unusual cold! Big Edie suggested that I sleep downstairs in the dining room. I moved my stretcher out of the Eye Room. I had slept there before when Little Edie had gone to New York City last December to have her eye operation. I was spending the winter in The Berkshires for a change, but after Big Edie and I talked on the telephone, I returned to East Hampton and spent New Years Eve at Grey Gardens, and remained there for a few days after Little Edie came back. The operation on one eye was a great success, and the eye recovery in Big Edie's bedroom went along perfectly.

I spent the night in the dining room as planned. The temperature was about eight degrees outside. Even with the cool atmosphere, I decided to return to the Eye Room tomorrow night, as the cat smell bothered me, the raccoons and rats were too playful, and, of course, I had to go all the way upstairs to use the bathroom. Some of the cats liked to sleep on the three sectional green couches that were placed around the room and they used them as other cats would use a litter box. Someone I knew in 1972 intended to remove the couches from their home as they expected to buy a new couch, and take the old ones to the dump heaps. Since the Beales didn't have any furniture in the dining/living room, except for a large table and four straight chairs, I had them brought here. It really wasn't too good an idea, as Brooks had to clean them all the time and the odor lingered.

After I had made up the stretcher, I went upstairs to say good night to the Beales and wish them a happy Christmas Eve. It was an unfortunate move on my part, as I returned to discover a puddle in the middle of the blanket covering the cot. It was a presentation from one of the cats. Did they think it a gift, or did they not want me to stay in my room? I'll never know, but I decided not to sleep downstairs again.

We had no Christmas tree or anything. A tree would not only be expensive, but it would be a dangerous fire hazard. A dozen cats or more pulling at a tree wouldn't be too sensible.

We did have Christmas presents to exchange, and cards that the Beales tacked on their bedroom walls.

Thursday, December 25, 1975

CHRISTMAS DAY

Everyone was up early, ready for breakfast, and feeling cheerful. Later, I went into Big Edie's room.

"Merry Christmas!" I placed my gifts on the bed. Jacqueline's presents from The Newtown Grocer were scattered all over a dresser top, guarded by a couple of cats.

"Good morning, Lois, and Merry Christmas!" the Beales chorused. "Your gifts haven't been wrapped yet," Big Edie said. "Oh, isn't that beautiful paper you used! Don't let the cats on them, Edie. Edie! I'll open them later, Edie! Put Lois's presents in a *safe* place, *no*, not there! Yes, that's better. Well, put them down! We can't open them now! We have to feed the kittens! Lois, take a box of chocolate mints from Jacqueline's box. I *insist*! Look at all the candy!"

"Thank you... Now, don't forget to open the presents!"

Little Edie looked delighted. "Oh, Lois, your wrapping paper is terrific! I'm going to use it to cover the tabletop in the hall. It's just the correct color for the hall! Don't worry; your Christmas gifts from us will be forthcoming this afternoon. We have so much to do. God!"

Big Edie, Little Edie, and I did open all our gifts a few hours later, except for one or two of hers that Big Edie decided she would unwrap at another time, as she liked gift-wrapped boxes so much. I could understand that.

Doris Francisco gave lovely presents to the Beales, and gave me a cross made of wood, blessed by the priest, that I still have. Slippers from Big Edie... and I don't recall now what Little Edie gave me... perhaps a scarf or blouse.

About 4:00 PM, part of the ceiling in the kitchen-studio fell! A big raccoon looked down at me through the hole, and then left, as if I bored him. The Beales' bathroom is over that part of the kitchen, and water from their basin had poured onto the studio floor. I placed newspapers down, now only a steady drip, drip, of water landing on the papers. I don't care for the hole, but the pipes will prevent a raccoon from getting through. It's cold this way, however, and I hope Brooks can fix it somehow. I reported all this to Little Edie while she was decorating the hall with wrapping paper and some fake greens. She didn't seem to care much, but Big Edie said she would attend to it. I am glad of that. With the cold, I need fresh air in the kitchen-studio, as it's really a terrible smelly cavity in the ceiling.

There were Some Christmas gifts for the Beales on the front porch. We didn't hear or see anyone leave them, but they are from the Maysles.

Early evening, a knock on the front door, and I answered it. Once again, Little Edie ran into her mother's bedroom. A Christmas turkey dinner in the same wicker basket used for Thanksgiving! It was from the Tobins. They must be thoughtful people.

Except for the ceiling, we all had a wonderful Christmas.

The electric did go off upstairs. Big Edie will be busy getting the house back "in order" tomorrow.

Many phone calls today, I know Doris Francisco on the wire a long, long time. Big Edie's son, Phelan, phoned from Oklahoma. After that, Al Maysles telephoned.

The Beales will certainly have a lot of extra food this week… and they need it.

Friday, December 26, 1975

It was much warmer, but it did rain all day. For some reason, the oil burner went off early this morning, and will not work. Big Edie phoned Schenck Oil and a repair truck arrived with two men. By noon, the oil-burner running, and it seems better than before it stopped working.

Doris Francisco called, and this time I talked with her also.

No Brooks.

Sunday, December 28, 1975

Someone telephoned and said that "a takeoff book" about the Beales mentioned in the East Hampton Star. It is published by Stein & Day and written by a man that owns BookHampton, a bookstore on Newtown Lane. The names are all changed and it's written like fiction, but you just *know* it's the Beales.

I wanted to buy it; however, the Beales don't want it brought into the house. I told them, "I will read it in the car," and they agreed to that.

I hope Brooks arrives tomorrow to repair the kitchen-studio ceiling!

Monday, December 29, 1975

I obtained *Gristmill*, written by George Caldwell.

Doris Francisco appeared as expected around 12:30 PM, and remained about an hour. She went upstairs into Big Edie's room and met her. They acted as if they had known each other for centuries, and were getting together again. Doris didn't seem to notice anything unusual about the room, her attention so centered on Big Edie. I could feel the Love there when I entered, after their private conversation had ended. Doris went downstairs with me.

Brooks had arrived, but he didn't do much except take the trash out. I introduced him to Doris, and he seemed surprised to find another woman in the house, a friend, and not someone connected with the Maysles film, or an interviewer. Little Edie didn't treat her as if she thought her a spy, so I knew Brooks was puzzled about Mrs. Don Francisco Jr. No friends of the Beales ever entered Grey Gardens now.

Doris drove me into town and we went to the bookshop. I asked for *Gristmill*. The author came up from the basement, a Mr. Caldwell. He gave me the book, after I had talked with him a few minutes, and wrote inside it, "To Mrs. Beale, Miss Beale, and Lois Wright with affectionate support for their way of life. George Caldwell... December, 1975." Doris obtained a book also, and he wrote something in it. We left the shop.

I returned alone to Big Edie's room, and read aloud the inscription George Caldwell had written.

"Take that book outside, Lois! I will not read one word!" Little Edie shouted and stamped her feet. "How could you bring that in *here*, I wouldn't even consider looking at it! Lois, you *must* leave this room!"

"I don't see why you are so upset, why you haven't read it, Edie. Mr. Caldwell gave it to us."

"Well, I am *upset*! We don't intend to read it, do we, mother?! Tell her!" Little Edie stamped her foot again, and the cats watched with alarmed expressions. "Tell her, Mother, before I throw this lamp at her!"

"Lois," Big Edie said pleasantly, "You can read the book in the kitchen, but don't bring it upstairs. We would rather not read it, but you may."

"All right, I'll do that," I said quickly and left their room. It proved to be the best arrangement. I read *Gristmill* that night, and realized the ending might bother them, but it was an amazing novel. I never suggested again that they read it. I wondered how the Beales knew they shouldn't read it... their E.S.P. certainly working. It gave me an odd feeling, reading *Gristmill* all alone, at the kitchen-studio table, hearing the Beale voices upstairs, and wondering just what would really happen here someday... I closed my mind on that question, as I often did. It was better not to know... not to think of Little Edie ever being alone. Without the Beales, I would have no desire to remain in East Hampton... What would I do?

Later, I went slowly upstairs. It seemed quiet in the hall and I felt sad. Black Cat watched me until after I had closed my door. By now, I, too, was a part of the old house, but the old house didn't need me, only the Beales, and no one else. It just accepted me; it didn't own me, as it did them.

My room was ice cold, but I fell asleep quickly. It was impossible to worry; some of the ghosts were so reassuring.

Wednesday, December 31, 1975

NEW YEAR'S EVE

Brooks arrived and fixed the kitchen-studio ceiling. It's only a temporary job, but it will "have to do" for now. At least, we can start off the New Year without the drip, drip, drip on the floor, and a raccoon watching me all the time.

This afternoon, I met Doris under the bridge for coffee, and enjoyed seeing her. She looked casual, but quite stunning at the same time. People always stared at Doris. Like Big Edie, she had a fine sense of humor, and her low, dramatic voice made all her statements interesting.

I drove back to Grey Gardens. Jacqueline's check had arrived at the bank in East Hampton. Now, something could be paid on the Newtown Grocery bill.

Big Edie, Little Edie, and I had a quiet, dignified New Year's Eve, with nothing to drink. We talked about the past year, and what the movie release in a theater in New York City, all over the country, and around the world, would mean to our life at Grey Gardens. Perhaps next year, the Beales could buy a car, and really fix up the house the way they wanted. Big Edie said she wanted "to buy a piano." The Beales believed they would receive 40 percent of the film profits "up front." Big Edie sang for us, and by 10:00 PM, I had retired. The Beales intended to stay up until midnight, and listen to music on their small Sony transistor radio that Jacqueline had once given them. They used it often, Brooks and I would get new batteries and Big Edie would be concerned until the Sony started working correctly again. She always heard the opera on Saturdays.

JANUARY 1976

Thursday, January 1, 1976

The New Year started in an uneventful manner. Most of the conversation revolved around the cold weather, the drafts in the house, the state of the world in general, the best countries to live in, and the personalities of the new kittens.

I was quite cold at night in the Eye Room, and on the "cot", wore slacks, cotton turtleneck sweater with a sweater over that, socks, and a wide-brimmed felt hat. A glass containing water had a good supply of ice on top of it by morning. When I entered a room, I judged its temperature by my breath. If I didn't see it, then the room would not be too frigid!

Big Edie's bedroom was always warm, too warm, I thought. Also, the sleeping cats on the beds provided loads of warmth. I would only remain in the Beales' room about five or ten minutes, due to the "close air" and heat.

Saturday, January 10, 1976

This afternoon, I attended a meeting of the Daughters of the American Revolution at St. Luke's Church in East Hampton. The Beales didn't seem too pleased about it, as they never liked me to get involved with a group of people.

Little Edie thought they would gossip about Grey Gardens, ask questions.

I didn't care about a "social life," and didn't want to become friendly with anyone, as it would only be a nuisance. However, I had received an invitation, as a member of the chapter, I decided to just "make an appearance" there.

I returned with homemade cookies and small cakes for Big Edie, so I was "forgiven" for attending, and I didn't stay too long.

"Lois, how can you tolerate those snobs?!" Little Edie demanded. "What did you do? Talk about me?! We can expect another raid, Mother!"

"The cookies look delicious," Little Edie commented. "I'll have some later, put them on the dresser."

Of course, I didn't talk about the Beales, and if their names were ever brought up, I always complimented them highly, but Little Edie would never believe that, perhaps it was because she chatted in a most unflattering way about me, at least I thought so.

Monday, January 12, 1976

There was heavy snow yesterday evening and early this morning. All the roads covered except for the main highway. Big Edie asked me to snap pictures with her camera and from the upstairs porch and also around the downstairs front porch area. Grey Gardens looked lovely and I remained on the grounds for an hour or more. Little Edie and I carried the trash bags through the snow to Lily Pond Lane. It was fun doing it together. Then, Edie quickly returned inside.

I dressed to go to Riverhead, as I had an appointment at the County Center. Big Edie talked to Doris, and asked if she could drive me there. Any trip further than Southampton was too much for my car, also I might get lost. The roads have changed so much in recent years. A throughway that I had not driven alone on and didn't want to, as I might end up in Queens! Horrors! It was difficult to find the way to Riverhead without getting on the parkway. All the signs pointed to the huge throughway as the "powers that be" wanted me to get on it. The Beales were concerned about the long journey, about 30 miles.

Doris Francisco arrived, and Little Edie waved at her and locked me out. It was a real luxury to sit in Doris's warm, clean car and relax on the comfortable large seat. A pity Big Edie couldn't enjoy a pleasant drive sometime, but it was difficult for her to leave the second floor of the old house. She would have to be carried down the stairs, and placed gently into an auto.

"Hello, Doris! I really appreciate your driving me to Riverhead. I hope the roads will be all right. Are you going to take that awful throughway?"

"*Never!* I don't like throughways, Lois."

I felt rather happy and said that we had to be very careful around Hampton Bays if we expected to stay on the Montauk Highway. The roads were treacherous, but Doris was a fine, careful driver, and we didn't have any trouble.

While in Riverhead, after my appointment, we stopped at Howard Johnson's for a hamburger and milkshake. Doris bought a small box of chocolates for Big Edie. She would expect something to be brought back from the trip and somehow Doris sensed this. I knew the Beales felt they deserved an "out-of-town" treat for having to worry about us. As time went on, I realized that Doris had a vast amount of perception concerning the Beales of Grey Gardens.

Saturday, January 17, 1976

My mother, Kathryn Erdmann Wright's wedding anniversary, and also Edith Bouvier Beale's wedding anniversary. Both occasions happened in New York City, but not the same year. They would talk about it over the telephone.

From my log for this date: "The house has turned extremely cold, even Big Edie's room. It's the wind and grey skies. Big Edie in a disagreeable humor... unusual. Perhaps she is not feeling well, or her bedroom isn't warm enough. Little Edie was quiet.

About 4:00 PM, I drove into town and returned with fish and ice cream.

Sunday, January 18, 1976

Cold, temperature 4 degrees at 7:00 AM, according to the Sag Harbor radio station. It is too chilly to write in my log book.

Monday, January 19, 1976

Down to six degrees. Two days in a row of near-zero temperatures. Doris Francisco phoned. My face bothers me, red and feels hot. It was frostbitten or frozen in the Eye Room while I was sleeping on the stretcher-cot. From my head down, I was warm and didn't wake up as my face slowly became numb. Doris wanted to drive me to the medical group in East Hampton this afternoon, after meeting me under the bridge, but I decided not to go. I do look odd.

Little Edie was delighted and excited. She received a telephone call from London while I was out. Some kind of interview program. Edie talked with Peter Wallace of the *London Times* about the movie. We had almost forgotten about it. Big Edie didn't care to speak on the broadcast via the phone, as she was too chilly.

Not quite as cold tonight, but I certainly can clearly see my breath in the Eye Room. Decided to paint for a while in the kitchen-studio. Working on an ocean scene now.

Thursday, January 22, 1976

I woke up to discover a heavy snowfall with ice on top of it. Didn't even try to start the car, no garage here. "Your poor tiny Karmann Ghia," Little Edie said. She looked pleased. Sometimes she was glad to see that I had problems, too. I can understand that and it amused me. Her smile was so pleasant. She was really sorry about it and pleased at the same time. "Do you think it's ruined?"

"I don't know, but I have extra food."

"Mother would give you some of our food, Lois. We have some bread and milk you could have."

"Thank you, I have some soup. I don't need anything. I'm going to paint on your portrait today, the one I promised Doris. What a winter!"

"Why, Lois, it's almost summer!"

We heard on the radio that gale warnings in effect. The wind started to really blow at 1:30 PM. The Sag Harbor station announced that the temperature would drop to zero tonight! I feel all the drafts from the wind in the kitchen-studio. 2:45 PM now and the wind is really howling! All this frightening weather with a clear sky today, but I do fear the cold, dark night with this screaming wind. My hands are cold and I have my black cowboy hat on all the time.

We all managed to live until morning, as we didn't freeze in our sleep.

Friday, January 23, 1976

I couldn't take photos for Big Edie this morning, because my fingers were too cold. It was below zero last night and it's zero now.

Doris telephoned the Beales, and then called me later. She asked if I cared to go out. I certainly did! Low on food and coffee. Thoughtful of her. My car started, but I couldn't get out from the driveway because of the snow.

Doris arrived with her Connecticut storm clothes on. I opened the back door and Doris walked into the studio. She wanted to see the portrait of Little Edie, it still needs work. The title is "Edith Bouvier Beale 2, The Dancer Waiting for Fame." Little Edie likes it and Big Edie is enthusiastic about the painting. I have vines and leaves in it, and you can't help but wonder if Edie will emerge from the vines, or if she will withdraw, recede into them, and remain at Grey Gardens.

I drove to the I.G.A. grocery store with Doris, and then under the bridge for coffee and toast.

Monday, January 26, 1976

The January thaw has arrived, and we are all delighted with the warm weather. A great deal of mud outside, the snow is melting.

Brooks appeared today to repair the refrigerator door, which wouldn't close. The raccoons may have been tampering with it. After that job, Brooks placed new batteries in Big Edie's radio, and then mopped the bedroom floor and the upstairs hall floors. He certainly is a wonderful help. As usual, after his chores, Brooks sat in the Beales bedroom and they talked a while before Big Edie gave him his check. Sometimes, Little Edie would be in a playful mood and hit Brooks in the stomach with her fist when he was standing, ready to leave.

"Oh, Edie! Don't do that to Brooks," Big Edie said. "Why do you do that?"

Little Edie laughed. "He's a boxer, Mother, didn't you know? In Florida. He told me all about it, didn't you, Brooks? I'm not hurting him. Would you like a Twinkie cake?"

Brooks smiled, "No, thank you, Miss Edie, I'll just take my check. I have to leave now, as Roberta is waiting for me. I did box in Florida, but I'm out of condition now."

Little Edie continued to be amused. "You look in good shape to me, Brooks old kid… here's your check. Is it enough? Lois can lock you out."

Later, I returned upstairs as Big Edie wanted to tell me something. One kitten was born last night, just one! It's black, and she wanted to give it to me. She knew that I like black cats. I never knew the Beales to give a kitten away before, but, of course, it would remain at Grey Gardens unless I left. We decided to name it Mason. Little Edie appeared puzzled about it all, and didn't look pleased.

David Maysles telephoned. He will arrive Wednesday with publicity people and a photographer.

Wednesday, January 28, 1976

Late this afternoon, David and Al Maysles drove into the grounds and parked in the mud. Little Edie had forgotten to warn them. No one else arrived, so a change in plans. They brought cameras.

Soon the downstairs front hall resembled a movie set with camera equipment, lights, and long, thick electric cords on the floor. It reminded us of the days when *Grey Gardens* was being filmed. The Beales were always apprehensive that the Maysles brothers would set the house on fire. It was their greatest worry in regards to the filming. The telephone rang. It was a call for David from London. Little Edie found something interesting to wear. The Maysles spent quite a while taking stills of Edie, and she enjoyed the attention. They didn't take any pictures of Big Edie. By the time that they were ready to leave, it was dark out.

The Maysles discovered that they couldn't go anywhere. Their red car had sunk deep into the mud, all their efforts were useless. I tried to help, couldn't and felt sorry for them. Downstairs, David telephoned some garages, but didn't seem to get a tow truck for some reason. We all gathered in Big Edie's room to consult with her. Big Edie's pleasant expression turned serious as she dialed a garage without referring to the yellow pages. We explained that the garages must be closed by now. Mrs. Edith Bouvier Beale paid no attention to us and soon had a mechanic on the line. Within twenty minutes, the Maysleses' car had been pulled from the mud by a Chick Phillips garage truck. It did cost $25, but it was worth it.

David and Al have to fly to Georgia tomorrow for some film work.

Thursday, January 29, 1976

About 4:30 this afternoon, I returned from town to find Doris sitting in the upstairs hall with an attractive priest. They were sitting on small chairs by the round painted-metal table with Little Edie. Doris introduced Father Grisay and mentioned they had known each other a long time in Connecticut.

Big Edie was tired and remained in her room. I don't really know if they had been in to see her or not.

I sat down for a while, and after some light conversation, Doris and Father Grisay left. I wondered why Doris had brought him to Grey Gardens, but Little Edie only talked about how she likes good-looking priests.

Friday, January 30, 1976

At least fifteen kittens have been born here in the last couple of days, all inbred for many generations. They have strange feet, an extra toe or small paw. The cats are fascinating because of the inbreeding and, due to this, I feel there is something of Pharaoh's Egypt in them.

Perhaps they can communicate with the Great Cats of old Egypt, and are somehow bewitched. Their eyes are different than housecats', and they certainly mate in an unusual way: they are quiet about it!

The Beales believe they are quite valuable, and I am inclined to agree with them, but we avoid discussing magic.

Saturday, January 31, 1976

There are twenty kittens at Grey Gardens at last count.

Celebrity magazine had a long write-up about the film *Grey Gardens*.

FEBRUARY 1976

Monday, February 2, 1976

Doris Francisco continues to talk at length with the Beales every morning on the telephone. She chats with me also for a short period.

All last night, the winds whistled around the mansion, with gale forces coming off the Atlantic. We felt the cold again. The weather was too awful to carry the trash bags out, so they are stacked in the upstairs hall, much to the delight of the rats. The Ghia's car door is frozen shut, and sheets of ice cover the poor auto.

This afternoon, I had to sketch ballet slippers with a black ballpoint pen and a purple pencil for the sign that the Maysles have that I made: "Edie the Great Dancer." They intend to place the slippers on the sign somehow.

Little Edie came into the kitchen-studio to see "what [I am] up to." I never knew how Edie was going to start a conversation; she is not a bore!

"Lois... I think Doris Francisco is a *spy*, a friend of Lee Radziwill, don't you think so?"

"I don't know... they best spy is one you don't suspect... but I don't know *who* she is... Big Edie may know."

"Oh, Mother wouldn't tell me. She's French, a Bouvier."

Little Edie looked puzzled. "I like Doris, but something's funny here. Well, you certainly are no help, as usual."

"How do you like the sketch I'm doing?"

"You should design shoes… Mother said to tell you to leave the tap water dripping tonight. It's going to be below zero. I should be in Florida now. I told Mother to buy a house there, but she wouldn't do it. She loves East Hampton. I hate it! God!"

"I wouldn't go to Florida at gunpoint!"

"Oh, that's because you paint. You don't know what's good for you. Why don't you get married?"

"No… I don't want to."

"You need a *man*, can't you understand, Lois, dear? I'm going to get one. Wow!"

"Rather you, than I."

"Well, you have too much talent, that's why you have *no* sense! I have to help Mother with the kittens now. Didn't anyone ever tell you to find a man?" Little Edie smiled.

"When I was five years old, I said that I didn't care to get married, but I would have married Larry Pool."

"I know. Isn't life *sad*?" Edie left the room.

Tuesday, February 3, 1976

Got up at 7:00 AM and went into the kitchen-studio, or rather, I just looked in. Pouring water from all over the ceiling! Horrible! Floors, table, chairs, all my papers and things wet, also the ballet slipper sketch! I dashed upstairs and informed the Beales. Little Edie got up and inspected the kitchen.

"God! It's only water, Lois. This has happened before. Open the door… I'll get a mop."

The large tub in Big Edie's bathroom had run over. Dirty water! Little Edie had left both taps running, and she hadn't removed all the cats' newspapers from with the tub, so the water didn't drain. I don't believe the tub drained anyway, as the Beales couldn't use the tub at all. Only the cats.

I managed breakfast standing by a gas stove, but my feet were soaked right through to my leather shoe-boots.

Later, I drove into town, as the car door had unfrozen. I hoped that Brooks would arrive today and work in the kitchen. I stopped at the post office and mailed the limp, wet sketch to David Maysles at his New York City studio. Collected the Beale mail, and returned home.

Monday, February 9, 1976

This has been quite an eventful day for us, as it included a U.F.O. sighting.

The activity started at 3:00 AM, when Little Edie woke me up. She had called the police, as she thought there was someone in the attic. Edie investigated, while I stayed on guard by Big Edie's room. She couldn't find anyone upstairs, so we didn't let the police inside. They looked around the grounds. The Beales decided it might have been a bear… nothing important, so we went back to sleep.

At 2:00 PM, I left for the post office to mail a letter to Jacqueline from her aunt. An envelope there from Big Edie from 1040 Fifth. I returned to Grey Gardens. The letter was from Nancy Tuckerman. She wrote that Jackie will pay for "perpetual care" for the Bouvier graves in East Hampton, and has informed Father Huntington.

Just after dinner, Little Edie rushed into the kitchen.

"Lois! There is a U.F.O. outside! I just told Mother."

I jumped from the chair. "Where is it?!"

"Over the porch, near the beach. We can see it from the upstairs porch. Hurry!"

Little Edie and I raced to the viewing area, shouting to Big Edie about the flying saucer.

"Be careful, girls!" Big Edie called back.

The cats seemed calm, and sat around near the walls, perhaps meditating. We stepped out onto the porch, and felt the cool night air. There were U.F.O.s, but they were not saucers. I could see a huge, round, bright orange light. It looked as large as the setting sun, but it wasn't the sun, and it didn't give off illumination. There were smaller round orange "balls" around it. Little Edie watched through her binoculars. The large one flew up and down, while the others circled. They moved as fast as "the wink of an eye," and then would slow to a hovering position. Little Edie offered the binoculars.

"No, thank you, it might hurt my eyes."

"Oh, you!" Little Edie said, putting the glasses back to her eyes. "Isn't this thrilling?!"

"But I am going to see if I can use my mind to ask them to come closer to us."

"All right, Lois… Go ahead."

I concentrated… The small ones receded about that time, and, much to my surprise, the huge one started to move forward, towards the porch. I could feel and see its pulsation.

"God! It's coming closer!" Edie laughed nervously. She opened the screen door and stepped inside.

I stayed outside a minute longer. I felt that the orange globe would envelop me and I would never be the same again. I thought I was ready, but then I felt frightened of the unknown. I was sorry, but I couldn't help it.

The globe seemed to realize this and politely went back to its original position over the beach as I slipped inside the safety of the old house.

"I saw it!" Little Edie said. "I'm going to get Mother into the rolling chair, so she can see it, and I think this should be reported to the police!"

"A good idea, Edie." I felt excited. "Just think, people from another planet, watching us. Isn't it great?!"

Big Edie, slightly annoyed about the entire matter, left her bed to sit in the rolling chair. Little Edie phoned the police, but received no important information, only that other calls had come in about it.

"The government will not allow them to tell us *any*thing," Little Edie commented as we all observed the orange objects from the hall window.

"Yes... I see it... but not too well... now I want to go back to my room. *Edie!* I'm speaking to you; take me back."

"All right, Mother, I think they are leaving now, they look dimmer."

"Edie, if you don't want to take me into the bedroom this minute, I'm going to run you over with this chair!"

The Beales returned to their room and locked the door for the night. The U.F.O.s had been around for about a half hour.

Tuesday, February 10, 1976

This morning, the Sag Harbor radio station mentioned the sightings yesterday evening. The Coast Guard said they were not U.F.O.s, only flares over the ocean. Guess they had to deny it.

Susan Froemke of the Maysles office telephoned to ask Little Edie to please wear makeup for the new opening of *Grey Gardens*. She forgot last time. The film will premiere at The Paris Theatre on February 20th. The Maysles would like Edie to appear in New York City on February 18th, and they have reserved a suite at the Plaza Hotel for her. David and Al requested that Little Edie should be able to see The

Paris Theatre, with her and her Mother's names in lights, from the Plaza suite window. The moviemakers really did something this time!

Little Edie hung up the pantry phone, and then went into the V.M.I. song with much dancing and stamping of her feet. "We all march together!" Edie shouted.

"I wish I could go."

"Well, you can't! You have to stay here with poor Mother. You want to ruin my *career?* Is that what you want to do, ruin my career?"

"No… but Brooks will be here to take care of Big Edie, he's going to spend the nights in the hall."

"My Mother cannot be left alone in this house with Brooks one minute! You have to watch him every second, or he will steal my clothes, and God knows what else!" Edie looked like she was going to cry.

"I don't think he would take anything, and he loves Big Edie."

"No! I can't leave Brooks alone here. Mother would never permit it! Besides, he has to go back and forth to his house to check up on Alberta, while he's staying here. Anyway, Brooks is interested in me, didn't you know?"

Wednesday, February 11, 1976

I saw Doris Francisco this afternoon, and talked with her about the opening. Doris said a friend of hers, John Clark, would drive us in to New York City, if Big Edie decided that I could go.

This evening, I started another painting. My impression of February 9th, the orange round glow in the sky over the beach. I wanted to get my mind off the coming excitement of the movie premiere, and if I could attend it or not. I *am* in the film for a short while, and would like to see the movie on a regular screen in a theater, instead of the small film shown at Grey Gardens. I did feel that I would miss some fun.

For the first time, there was tension in the house. Not too much, but it was there.

We are all wondering and worrying about Brooks. He has no phone and we haven't seen him recently. He *has* to be here when Edie leaves to take care of Big Edie, and feed the cats and raccoons. I could never do all that and said so numerous times.

Friday, February 13, 1976

This morning, Big Edie wanted me to go to the post office early, so I couldn't help Little Edie with the trash bags. Most important that I mail a letter to Brooks, asking him to telephone the Beales about making arrangements to stay here while Edie is in New York City. There is no other way to reach him! I broke all speed limits getting into town.

This afternoon, I mentioned to Big Edie that I would like to attend the opening on February 20th. I could go in on the same day, and return that night.

"I have been invited by the Maysles," I said.

"Well, you might not be invited here, then." Big Edie's grim expression alarmed me slightly, and Little Edie shouted, "No, I'll *never* speak to you again if you leave on the 20th!"

"*Why not?!* It's only *one* day! Perhaps Alberta could stay here with Brooks also?" It was my turn to glare.

Little Edie lowered her voice to a whisper. "I don't want Alberta. It's bad enough having Brooks roaming around the house while I am away. You know they would both grab my clothes."

"We'll see, Lois." Big Edie looked less severe.

"Anyway, we don't have time to talk about it now, as I have to operate on Doris's dress."

"What are you going to do to it?" I knew Doris had given Edie a beautiful designer gown that she had worn at the Westport Playhouse in Connecticut. Purple and shocking pink, a Grecian cut, with a scarf to match.

"Oh, you know… I have to rearrange everything. I might have to borrow your scissors, Lois. But the gold slippers Doris gave me are perfect!"

I left the bedroom thinking there still might be a chance that I could go in to see the movie. I had no idea how long it would play in New York City, and thought in terms of a week or two.

Saturday, February 14, 1976

This morning, I gave each Beale a tiny box of chocolates for Valentine's Day. Big and Little Edie had a valentine card for me, and a large valentine card to be mailed today to Jacqueline.

Later, the phone started ringing. First, Doris Francisco, then someone connected with the movie, telling Little Edie that she might have to appear on a TV talk show on the 18th, an interview by Pat Collins. Brooks telephoned and said he would stay here day and night while Edie visited in New York City, as long as she didn't disappear more than a few days.

"Brooks," Big Edie answered, "if my daughter remains in that city longer than three days, then she better buy a steamship ticket to France, 'cause she can't come back here! No, Brooks, don't laugh, I mean it, so don't worry. Edie isn't ready for Paris yet."

"Oh, Mother, I'm always ready for Paris!"

"Ready in a year or two, more like two hundred! What would happen to your cats?"

"Isn't it awful, I'm just a guest at my Mother's house." Little Edie glanced at me and smiled. "I would miss my cats."

"What about your Mother?" Big Edie said goodbye to Brooks and hung up the telephone.

"I would miss Mother, she's very intelligent and entertaining, a Bouvier." Little Edie sighed.

"Are you going on the Pat Collins talk show in New York?" I asked, and opened the bedroom door to go downstairs.

"I guess so. The Maysles want me to. God!"

"All right, Edie. I'll wait until you return from the opening, before I go in with Doris to see the movie, but I don't want to miss it!"

The Beales smiled. I felt rather guilty about worrying them, and they knew it.

Sunday, February 15, 1975

I gave Big Edie the *Sunday Times* with the *Grey Gardens* film ad in it. The paper is only delivered weekdays because the Beales thought it cost too much on a Sunday. It was difficult enough paying for it now.

Tuesday, February 17, 1976

Little Edie said she is leaving tomorrow on the Hampton Jitney. It's a minibus.

Another ad for *Grey Gardens* in The Times and also a long quote by Peter York of the *London Sunday Times*.

Many phone calls between the Maysles and the Beales.

I met Doris under the bridge and talked with her. Said I couldn't leave here now.

Wednesday, February 18, 1976

Woke up about 7:00 AM to hear Brooks knocking on the door. The Beales just woke up. Too late for the Jitney Bus. I let Brooks inside, and then had breakfast. Edie decided to take a 1:00 PM train to Penn. Station, so I drove into town for groceries. A huge ad in the *Times* for *Grey Gardens*. I returned home. Heard that Doris is expected to drive Edie to the East Hampton Station.

After learning the latest News Flash regarding Edie's departure from the old house, David telephoned and was most upset! A television crew at The Plaza Hotel was waiting for Edie now. He intended to call Schaefer's Taxi and East Hampton and have his star brought into New York City right away. Little Edie agreed to this, but she wasn't too pleased, as she enjoys traveling alone on trains and buses. Recently, Edie had been saying, "He who travels alone, travels fastest."

Doris arrived, and I opened the front door for her. The cab arrived next, and we all shouted to Edie that "the taxi is here! Edie! The taxi!"

"I know!" Edie glided down the stairs, looked in the large dim hall mirror, and said goodbye to Doris, Brooks, and me, and went out to the waiting cab. "Close the door, and make certain all the locks are secure!" Little Edie ordered, her last thoughts being the safety of Grey Gardens.

Doris chatted a while with Big Edie, and then drove off.

Once again, Brooks brought in his "beat up" mattress and a small bed frame to place in the upstairs hall. He selected an area near the banister, a few yards from the Eye Room door. It seemed strange to be alone in the house without Edie, only Brooks to do all the many routine chores. I would have the responsibility of overseeing this, keeping Big Edie informed, trying to prevent apprehensive, that we could depend on Brooks for the next three days and nights.

However, our confidence began to dwindle and even diminished completely. Big Edie and I were "locked" in the mansion with an active drunk, and we had to use all our wits! The drinking started slowly, building to a crescendo. This evening, Brooks didn't act quite the same as usual and I had a chance to see what Big Edie thought. She suggested he might be taking some kind of pills for his health that affected him adversely. We conversed in low tones, not wanting to be overheard.

By the time Brooks went to bed in the upstairs hall, I decided it was alcohol. Earlier, he wanted to talk all the time, even following me into the kitchen-studio while I was having dinner. He didn't sit down.

"Brooks, I'm a hermit, not just a recluse, so I would like to be alone."

"You really are a hermit?"

"Yes."

"Well," Brooks said, leaning against the refrigerator door. "How would you like me to kill all the raccoons and rats for you and Mrs. Beale? I have a friend. He's black, and likes to skin raccoons and cats. Sells the pelts. Man! You should see what he can do with them!"

"Wait until Edie returns."

"Oh, I've asked her, but she said never mind. I could use traps and also a rifle, borrow a gun."

"No. Good night, Brooks."

"Well, I'm in charge of *security* here now. Have to watch for kidnappers. You know what happened to Patty Hearst?"

"Yes."

"You know what that black man was doing to her. Can't have that here."

"No, we can't."

"I have direct communications to the CIA, just in case. Don't you worry now."

"Oh, no, I'm not."

"Well, I'll see you in the morning, Miss Lois."

"Yes, good night, Brooks."

"Why can't I call you just 'Lois'? Why do I have to say Miss Lois, or Miss Wright?"

"You don't. Call me what you want to, but you better check the security now."

"All right, Lois, I'll do that." Brooks smiled. "Can't be too careful."

Thursday, February 19, 1976

Brooks spent last night in the upstairs hall, and he is drinking. Heard him walking around, and he wasn't too quiet about it. Also, he was talking to himself, but I couldn't hear what he was saying. No sound from Big Edie's bedroom, I guess she didn't want Brooks coming in. This morning, Doris telephoned and talked to Big Edie. She didn't allude to Brooks. We had hoped he would be sober this morning.

I had to be in Bridgehampton this afternoon for a few minutes, I didn't want to leave, as Brooks seemed worse and my car was not working right. However, I decided I had to go, but asked Jack Helmuth to drive me, as I didn't want to be delayed getting back by car problems. Jack arrived and then Brooks locked me out. He looked very drunk."

"I'll only be gone about half an hour," I told him. "Be sure you stay on the alert for my call to unlock the door."

I ran to Jack's car on Lily Pond Land and jumped in.

"We will have to hurry, Brooks is drinking!"

"He is?!"

"Yes, and Big Edie is alone with him, locked in the house. I would like you to come in with me when we return, so you can see him. He is on a real binge. But there is no one else we can get to take his place. No one else. It's Brooks, or no one, and he *is* still feeding the animals and trying to cook on the hot-plate, and mopping up. Big Edie wouldn't allow anyone else inside to work in her room."

Jack looked nervous. "I'll step inside, but I don't want to talk with him, can't tell how a drunk will react. I do have heart trouble and I am well over 70 years old."

"I know, Jack, I just want a witness to his condition, and also I want Brooks to see you."

On the way back from Bridgehampton, I made a fast stop for ice cream. We would need it, and I didn't intend to leave Grey Gardens again until Little Edie arrived home.

Brooks unlocked the back door for us. He had a camera in one hand. "If anyone tries to get in here, I'm going to take their picture and send it to the CIA. They don't know how smart I am. The kidnappers just don't know. In fact, *you* don't know. I'm really a secret agent."

Jack could see that Brooks was drunk. He left in a few minutes, and appeared quite concerned. I locked the door and went into Big Edie's room. We both knew that we would have to cope alone with a difficult situation. The movie hadn't even opened at the Paris Theatre yet, and all this was going on.

Brooks opened the door and came in. He was far from clean and neat, and smelt of alcohol. His words were slurred.

"I just fed the raccoons, one tried to bite me, but I got my hand out of the way just in time. I can move faster than those raccoons if I have to!"

Big Edie looked at Brooks intently. "I think you have been taking too many cough drops, Brooks. I can tell. Better not take so many from now on. Did you have a cold?"

"Yes, I did, Mrs. Beale, but I'll stop taking so many cough drops, I didn't realize…"

"Don't forget now: the cough drops don't agree with you."

"I'm your hospitalization man, Mrs. Beale. I'm taking care of you, and I don't need any more cough drops," Brooks laughed.

But I guess Brooks couldn't help it. He had to keep drinking; he was too far gone to stop now.

Friday, February 20, 1976

Almost all night long, right outside my door, Brooks was "sending and receiving" on a dead TV set he had brought into the house from his car. He was talking with other secret agents, he said.

About 3:00 AM, I heard Brooks in the upstairs porch room pounding with a hammer on the locks on the door, and then he went upstairs to do some pounding on the front door. I knew Big Edie heard him, but she, too, remained quiet.

At last, morning came. Poor Brooks, he would have a hangover. But he didn't, and he continued to drink instead.

Part of the upstairs electric went off about 8:00 AM. My room, the hall, and the Beales' bedroom! I discovered the refrigerator turned off, unplugged. Brooks must have had something else in the refrigerator's outlet, what, I didn't know. Anyway, I guess it blew out the electric. I dashed upstairs to tell Big Edie. Soon, the electrician, Al Stewart, and his son arrived. He took one look at Brooks and seemed shocked. Because of the emergency, Big Edie allowed Mr. Stewart into her room. He seemed frightened of Brooks and mentioned it to Big Edie. However, he repaired the electric. I walked out to West End Road and picked up the *Times* from the driveway. A huge, half-page or more ad for *Grey Gardens* was in the newspaper. Also, a review and the complete cast list. Film clips will be on TV tonight, etc. It's the world premiere of *Grey Gardens*.

We told Al Stewart about it, and to watch TV tonight. Big Edie and I wouldn't be able to. Al said he would watch, and then drove off.

Shortly, Brooks staggered out. He wanted to go home for a while to check on Alberta.

Big Edie was just picking up the phone when I walked in after locking Brooks out.

"Oh, hello, Jacqueline. How are you, dear?" Big Edie motioned me to stay. I listened to the conversation, and then Big Edie asked me to talk with Jacqueline on the phone. She asked about Brooks, and I said, "He is drunk, but he can still feed the cats." Jacqueline didn't seem to know what to do about it, and her aunt didn't ask her to do anything, so we changed the subject, and then I handed the phone back to Big Edie. She just seemed to want Jacqueline informed about Brooks, and mentioned his condition to her. They chatted about the movie. Jacqueline said she would be going to Paris for three days. After a while, they hung up, and I thought that Big Edie looked better. I asked her if she wanted some cream of pea soup, that I intended to heat some, and heaven knows when Brooks would be back, and since all the animals were fed, it didn't matter if he never appeared, unless he stopped drinking. Big Edie and I each enjoyed a large bowl of hot soup, toast, and cheese. So far, Little Edie hadn't been bothered or worried.

Later, Brooks knocked on the door, and I let him in. He came back, he said, "to guard the house tonight." Brooks continued his round-the-clock drinking. I didn't think Alberta wanted him home in such a state!

Saturday, February 21, 1976

Brooks was quiet during the night, and seemed better this morning. We expect Little Edie back this evening. While Brooks was cooking in the bedroom, I noticed a large empty gin bottle on top of his unmade bed. The hall was a mess. His clothes were tossed all around, the broken TV, and old suit-cases.

Little Edie telephoned and her mother told her to return right away. It was time to.

By early afternoon, Brooks had started to drink again. We will be glad to see Edie!

Someone brought Brooks's dog here, so he left to take it to his house. Big Edie asked him to.

Little Edie called again. The 4:00 something train had left Penn. Station, and she missed it, the last one.

"Well, you take a train, and then a cab to East Hampton. Just go as far as you can on the train. I'll pay for the taxi. I believe you get off at Speonk, now *do* that, Edie. I mean it! Brooks has been drinking and it's been very difficult for Lois and me."

Edie agreed to the plan.

Brooks returned and managed to do his work. He appeared calmer, but far from sober.

About 9:30 PM, Little Edie knocked on the front door. She had taken a cab from Speonk, the last train stop. She was "full of pep." We were not, and it wasn't too long before Big Edie wanted to rest and sleep. I was tired, but talked with Little Edie until nearly midnight. Big Edie had told Brooks to leave, and he had, with his bedding and things. Grey Gardens had returned to normal.

"Well, you and Mother certainly look awful!" Little Edie said. "Can't get along without me, can you?"

Tuesday, February 24, 1976

Little Edie had been home a couple of days and we were all happy. Yesterday, Edie was shouting on the telephone at the Maysles in New York City. They had called, and talked an hour, about other movie openings, and Edie didn't like something-or-other. Also, they want her to go back to the city for more interviews. I wish she didn't have to. Little Edie said she did one for Arlene Frances with David, and David mentioned me, but she shut him up.

We also found out that on the Jim Jensen TV news broadcast on Monday, they ran a few film clips of *Grey Gardens* and I was in one of them. Perhaps it was Sunday night.

Doris Francisco phoned. She had been away, busy with her son Peter. I met her in the village and talked about what Big Edie and I had been through.

Wednesday, February 25, 1976

The Beales asked me not to leave the house, as they expected a fan or two. They had received a call about it. One woman had a gift for Little Edie. She didn't want to see them, however.

At 2:30 PM, three people arrived on the front porch. They had driven all the way out from New York. I opened the door and talked to them a couple of minutes, as the Beales requested. To my surprise, they recognized me from the film! One young woman stepped forward and handed me a long boa made from many huge feathers! This was the gift to Little Edie. It looked rather old and most amazing. I thanked her and closed the door.

Little Edie had fun with the boa, and put it away somewhere. I could now drive into town. Thought about going to the Paris Theatre on Monday. The large ads are still in the *Times*.

About 4:00 PM, I returned. Al Maysles telephoned, as Little Edie was still angry at David.

It's been decided that I can go to New York this Monday.

Thursday, February 26, 1976

I talked with the Beales once again about March 1st. I said I would phone the Maysles for three free tickets. First, I telephoned Doris, and informed her that we could leave on Monday. At last! She said, "Fine." I then called the studio, and talked with Al. He said that Susan Froemke, one of the producers and editors would have three free tickets at the box office in my name. Perhaps she would be there. I hoped she would be at the Paris, as I had met Susan, and liked her.

Quite later in the afternoon, Al phoned. A new development, the Maysles want Little Edie in New York City for a huge press conference… on Monday! David on the phone, too. The Beales were upset, as they can't have Brooks "take over." Again, and I just can't stay in Big Edie's bedroom fixing meals on the hot-plate, staying with her, feeding the animals, cleaning the floors and everything. Big Edie didn't want anyone to leave her alone to go down into the kitchen. One person in the house could never leave the top floor while Little Edie is away, except to carry the box of groceries upstairs.

The Beales knew of no one else except Brooks they would allow in, and now Brooks couldn't return unless Little Edie was here, and the drinking had stopped. What a problem! There were many excited phone calls, and I was upset, too.

On Friday, we were all shouting about it in Big Edie's room, and I got so distraught that I ran out of the house, leaving the kitchen door wide open, an unheard-of thing to do. I returned about an hour or two later, and everyone was calm, but still worried.

Sunday morning, Doris said she would help, and the Beales accepted her offer.

This afternoon, a stunning young woman from *The Washington Post* arrived. She had an assistant with her, a man. After a while, Little Edie brought them into the bedroom, where they chatted with Big Edie. I was introduced. After their departure, I complimented the woman interviewer, but Big Edie thought she was "too thin." She believed women should have "a French figure."

Tonight, there was much thought, talk, and activity regarding Edie's trip to New York. Little Edie had to plan her clothing apparel and model it for her mother.

Doris telephoned again to say that she would arrive at daybreak tomorrow. With two people in the house, Doris could leave the upstairs and have coffee, etc. in the kitchen-studio, and she could use my bathroom where there were no cats.

Little Edie was awake most of the night, going through this and that, looking at papers and things.

MARCH 1976

Monday, March 1, 1976

Doris arrived at dawn. She had kept her word, and we were all relieved. A limousine soon materialized out of the fog, and Little Edie once again left for New York City. We expected her back late in the afternoon.

I went down into the kitchen for breakfast, knowing that Doris would be feeding all the cats and kittens, and at the same time, handing one thing or another to Big Edie. Once in a while, Doris managed to get into the kitchen-studio for a cigarette or a fast cup of coffee. By noon, she was getting tired.

"It's just like a hit in the gut!" Doris remarked about Big Edie's bathroom. She had to wash the dishes in there. She also found it impossible to cook eggs on the hot-place with the cats moving closer and closer to her. They knew they would be eating from Big Edie's dish, and were restlessly waiting. Sometimes, Little Edie had a favorite cat around her feet as well as on the bed, and by the "stove." It was difficult for Doris, but she stayed. She wore a hat, carried a small flashlight down the back stairs, and had boots on. I had mentioned what to bring with her. Doris ate her lunch quickly at the clean table in the kitchen and used my plates and things.

Big Edie was being quite charming, but also demanding. All the kittens had to be found and brought over to her. Water had to be heated so their tiny eyes could be wiped with a damp cloth. Big Edie also needed attention, help going in and out of the bathroom in the rolling chair, while she asked that certain male cats and certain female cats be separated. There was movement upstairs every minute until Big Edie decided to rest, and then they would talk.

When Doris appeared in the kitchen, I would have a cup of coffee ready for her, but occasionally she couldn't even drink it, before Big Edie called on the phone for her. The ring seemed to go right through you, striking all the nerves with a jolt, when Big Edie telephoned.

Doris heard, and then saw the heads of the raccoons in the refrigerator room. She notices a large black rat run quickly near the side of the kitchen wall, and crawl down a hole into the basement.

By late afternoon, Doris looked as if she had been through battle, tested by fire, and had successfully survived. She was sitting in the rolling chair, talking to Big Edie and me, when Little Edie returned. The star was excited; she had to go back tomorrow and Wednesday! A blow to us! Doris said she couldn't make it tomorrow.

Many phone calls tonight back and forth to the Maysles Studio. Once again I said I could not stay here alone doing all the jobs. David or Al offered me $50, but I couldn't accept it. I just couldn't do it, not even for $50 a day. I think the Maysles were angry at me. Big Edie said that I am allergic to cats, and I think that's the truth. Not one cat, but so many in one room, without air.

Tuesday, March 2, 1976

This morning at 6:30, a young woman named Deanna Douglas was admitted into the house by Little Edie. Deanna came upstairs and met Big Edie in her room. I locked Edie out and she drove off towards the city.

The Maysles had somehow convinced the Beales that a friend of theirs, Deanna, could be trusted, and could manage. They gave her $50 a day and she stayed all day. Big Edie rested, and didn't talk to her as she did to Doris. However, Deanna had to remain in the bedroom all the time, except for fast trips to the kitchen-studio. She had some food with her. I brought ice cream in around 5:00 PM and notice a bumper sticker on her car that stated "Cleanliness is Next to Godliness." I had to smile.

Shortly, Little Edie arrived. She had been interviewed again. On the way out, Deanna told me that she did have time to meditate and that it helped. Would come back tomorrow, as Little Edie seemed to be commuting now.

Big Edie seemed tired from being around a stranger all day. It was a strain.

Doris phoned and said she would be over around 5:00 PM Wednesday, as Little Edie expected to be gone longer on this trip.

Wednesday, March 3, 1976

The *Grey Gardens* ad is still running in *The New York Times*. After Deanna arrived, Little Edie drove away.

I seem to be getting a cold. It's all this disconcerting activity recently.

Deanna left a rather large violin case in the hall. I wondered what could be inside, and she said nothing about it. After Big Edie's lunch, Deanna brought the case into the bedroom, opened it, and soon had a violin in her hands. It was a relief to know it wasn't a machine gun or something. Deanna sat on Little Edie's bed, and played the instrument. It seemed to help Deanna's nerves.

Later, an interviewer telephoned from New York, and talked with Big Edie. He wanted her to sing "Tea for Two" on his program, right then. Deanna put down her violin and went to listen on another phone. I thought Big Edie sang very well, as usual. Shortly, she hung up the phone, and decided it was almost raccoon feeding time.

At 5:30 PM, Doris Francisco arrived on the front porch, and Deanna left in a hurry, carrying her violin case.

Little Edie returned this evening while Doris was still here, sitting in the rolling chair, talking with Big Edie.

Friday, March 5, 1976

I am trying to get over this cold. Yesterday, I spent the entire morning sleeping on the canvas stretcher. It's so strange to be ill in Grey Gardens. The Beales left me alone.

This afternoon, I went under the bridge for a milkshake. The ad in the *Village Voice* has a photo of my signs in it.

Saturday, March 6, 1976

I feel much better. The Beales expecting the Press today. It would be better if they could come here, instead of Edie having to leave! Doris will arrive this afternoon, just to have a cup of coffee and chat. I drove into town again.

I returned to Grey Gardens and noticed Doris's car. She unlocked the door for me. Then we locked Little Edie out. She was off to Guild Hall, a party for Ted Strong, Gould Strong's brother, an old lover of Big Edie's. Gould lived at Grey Gardens once. Little Edie returned via a cab, the photographers were here. Later, Doris departed.

While I was having an early dinner in the kitchen-studio at 6:00 PM, with W.O.R. on the radio, I unexpectedly heard Little Edie's voice. It was a recorded tape, and advertisement for the movie now playing at The Paris Theatre. I didn't know the film was advertised on radio and TV, told the Beales about it. I don't think Little Edie ever bothered to hear the ad. It was on again at 6:20 PM. For some time, the tape ran every evening. Well, around 6:00 to 7:00, the Beales are quite busy. I'm not.

Sunday, March 7, 1976

I went out for the thick Sunday Times. Another surprise, my name in the paper's *Grey Gardens* ad: "Signs by Lois Wright" near a reproduction of "The Great Singer" and "The Great Dancer" birthday signs I had painted.

Doris said she would have John Clark drive me into New York to the Paris Theatre tomorrow. How wonderful! Little Edie has stopped commuting!

Big Edie is not too happy about our going, as she worries about an accident or something, and then Doris and I would both be taken out of her life together. Little Edie didn't like her Mother upset; she would frown when the trip was mentioned, but she didn't say "No." She couldn't, as Big Edie said we could go, even if it caused her much concern. However, we were only to see the movie, have an ice cream soda in Schrafft's, and carefully drive right back to East Hampton.

I haven't been to Manhattan since 1963, and looked forward to the trip. Susan Froemke was informed of our arrival tomorrow.

Monday, March 8, 1976

A clear day, ready for the journey to New York City. Doris called early this morning.

Little Edie will be busy with newspaper interviewers, California and Chicago writers. Also, Father Huntington is expected.

Doris and John Clark arrived. The Beales were in the upstairs porch room and we said good bye there. Big Edie turned to Doris and said, "Why don't you change your mind and say, Babes, it's so lovely on the outside porch now." She knew I was not to be deterred. Doris smiled and told Big Edie she really wanted to drive in to see the film, as she had never seen it.

We left for Manhattan in Doris's comfortable car and didn't stop once. John left us off in front of the theater and parked nearby. We all went in free. I felt good vibrations and enjoyed the film, the 1:35 PM show.

John obtained the auto, we jumped in, and were soon leaving for Suffolk County. Doris didn't want to halt or hesitate until Riverhead. We had ice cream there, bought Big Edie candy, and in to time arrived back at Grey Gardens. Little Edie let us in.

Wednesday, March 10, 1976

I returned to my usual routine and painted a self-portrait on an old, round, tin tray. A dark blue background. It's something like a tintype. "Lois, the Ghost of Grey Gardens."

The Washington Post telephoned and talked with Little Edie mostly about cats.

Thursday, March 11, 1976

Edie left with Don, the driver of a black car, at dawn. Deanna Douglas arrived before Don. I got up and went down into the kitchen-studio. There is snow on the ground.

Doris arrived so that Deanna could leave at 2:00 PM. She had informed the Maysles that she couldn't stay any longer from now on.

Little Edie didn't return until nearly 11:00 PM! She was expected at 8:30. I locked Doris out about a quarter to midnight. She is a wonderful help.

Friday, March 12, 1976

Certainly glad the Edie is back! Much trash in the upstairs hall, and we carried it all out to the road. What a job!

It is a quiet evening here, with everyone relaxing.

A quote from the Mini-Reviews in the *New York Daily News*. It states this every day:

> *Grey Gardens* — 3 ½ stars (PG). The Aunt and Cousin respectively of Jacqueline Onassis share their most intimate thoughts and recollections with a probing camera. A very moving experience as two famous recluses emerge as indestructible, proud, and vibrant women.

Tuesday, March 16, 1976

It is pouring rain, a storm. Edie left for New York City about 6:00 AM. Deanna arrived to care for Big Edie and all the cats, twenty kittens that need attention. She changed her mind, and will remain here all day, until 5:00 PM.

Yesterday, Little Edie invited me to travel to France with her for the showing of the film. We could stay in my British sister-in-law's mother's house in Cannes. However, I didn't think we would ever go.

Deanna left at 5:30 PM, and no Edie. David phoned, Edie will arrive about an hour later, he said.

The oil-burner went off! I told Big Edie, and she called the repair people. They came immediately. I opened the basement doors for them and, after inspecting the burner, they said it's the fault of the heavy rains. The repair truck was still here when Little Edie returned from her trip about 8:00 PM. I met her outside, as Big Edie asked me to watch the servicemen from Schenck's Oil. This was all more important to Little Edie then her interviews in the city. The oil-burner went on.

Wednesday, March 17, 1976

Very cold out, and windy. After lunch, Edie said that Peter Beard telephoned from Montauk. He expects to arrive with William Holden, and Edie appeared enthusiastic, as she always liked his movies. She put on her red Lincoln Center dress, and even swept the long front stairs!

Brooks hadn't been around for some time.

Sadly, Peter Beard and William Holden never arrived, and didn't phone again. Poor Edie! However, she got busy with her jobs around 6:00 PM, and chatted with her mother, and the disappointment was soon forgotten.

Thursday, March 18, 1976

Many phone calls. Our Star will have to go into New York tomorrow to appear on *The Barry Farber Show*, and she is also expected to meet Andy Warhol for an interview. Doris and Deanna will appear here.

Friday, March 19, 1976

Little Edie left for New York on schedule, just after Deanna came in. She wanted to know when Doris would arrive, and I said, "About 5:00 PM, not to worry." Edie didn't leave today until 2:00 PM, but will not be able to get back until dawn! SO far, Edie really hasn't been paid for anything, perhaps a few dollars, the expenses are many. We will hear Edie on the W.O.R. Farber program tonight, if she gets safely into the city. One never knows. Big Edie always worries about her.

Doris came in at 5:00 PM, and we locked Deanna out. The Maysles had offered Doris $50 a day to stay in the house, but of course she refused, saying "she wouldn't do it for any price," only for her love of the great Mrs. Edith Bouvier Beale.

Talking about this matter at a later date, Big Edie told Doris, "You should have taken their check, Babes, then we could have divided it."

Doris cooked Big Edie's dinner in the bedroom, then she ate her dinner at the table in the upstairs hall, chopped meat I had cooked on the gas stove in the kitchen-studio. I ate there as usual.

As it neared time to retire, and Doris had fed all the many cats, kittens, and raccoons, she changed her clothes and removed the tall leather boots. I walked into Big Edie's room to find Doris resting on top of Little Edie's bed, looking something like her, with all the cats around. She was lying straight out on her back, conversing with Big Edie, who was on the other bed. It was about 8:30 PM. Doris had to get up to hunt for a stray kitten and I noticed she had along, brown monk's robe on with a hood. Very dramatic for the Grey Gardens night.

Big Edie asked her not to go into the upstairs hall, not even to my bathroom, as a bear or something might grab her, and to keep the door locked. I roamed the halls alone when I felt it necessary or convenient, and the Beales marveled that I would do this.

The Barry Farber Show came on the radio. The Maysles and Edie Beale, and later on, an interview with Peter Townshend of England. We listened intently to Edie, of course. Mr. Farber said he intended to telephone Mrs. Edith Bouvier Beale in East Hampton later in the show and talk with her on the air, and perhaps she would sing "Tea for Two."

The studio people got their call through, and Big Edie talked with Mr. Farber, and I think he thought she was most charming. Yes, she would sing "Tea for Two." He hung up, but would call back later, so we had to be on the alert for his next call. However, by the time he phoned again, Big Edie had gone to sleep. We woke Mrs. Edith Bouvier Beale up, and she chatted a while with her head resting on the pillow, and then, at his request, and after lifting herself higher in bed, sang "Tea for Two" over the network. I loved her for it. The job finished, Big Edie went back to sleep.

Later, we were all awake again, and heard a re-broadcast of the show.

Little Edie arrived home at 4:00 AM, and with the sun breaking, Doris drove to her house in the Northwest Woods in East Hampton.

Tuesday, March 23, 1976

Brooks returned, sober, and repaired the kitchen-studio ceiling. We were glad to see him in good condition again. From now on, he could work here, mopping floors and plugging rat-holes, etc.

Nothing of real interest has been happening lately. Telephone calls come in… Doris stops by once a day for a cup of coffee, and to visit for a short time in Big Edie's room.

Friday, March 26, 1976

Susan Froemke telephoned to tell the Beales that the Maysles are in Washington, D.C., and the film should open there soon.

Monday, March 29, 1976

Little Edie had to go into New York City to have luncheon with famous people, and another interview.

Doris arrived at 9:00 AM. Norm, the driver of the black car, drove in the grounds, and soon Edie was on her way.

I started a painting of Dracula. It just seemed to appear on the canvas, I hadn't planned the portrait.

Doris left around 1:00 PM, as Deanna appeared. Early evening, Deanna departed as Doris returned. About 11:00 PM, Miss Edith Bouvier Beale arrived at Grey Gardens. Little Edie seems just the same as before the movie was ever even first thought of. The Beales are not affected. The glare of publicity and its consequences have meant nothing to them.

April 1976

Thursday, April 1, 1976

Pouring rain all day. Little Edie walked into the kitchen-studio with a small shiny object in one hand.

"Lois, dear, this is the tin eye protector, or shield, that I wore in the hospital after my cataract operation." Edie placed in on the black table. "Could you paint an eye on it for me? I may want to wear it again when I have the other eye fixed."

I said I would do it, but it wasn't too good an idea, as the oils didn't dry. I had to give it to Edie "wet", and never saw the blue eye I had painted again.

This afternoon, while in town, I noticed a sale going on in a store that had to close. Rents too high, I was told. Anyway, I bought a "silver" baton for Little Edie, the kind you twirl and march with in parades.

Big Edie seemed to have more fun with it than her daughter, and twirled it in bed, looking pleased that she could. She was a wonderful sport, a person not to be forgotten. Later, the baton was displayed on the wall.

Friday, April 2, 1976

After dinner, while I was painting an ocean scene, NBC or CBS wanted to come here with their TV cameras, but Big Edie said, "No camera in the house now."

The April 5th *Village Voice* has a write-up about the Beales by Blair Sabol.

Big Edie seemed in a nostalgic mood, and reminisced. Her mother, Maude Sargeant Bouvier, died on April 2nd, and she still missed her.

Saturday, April 3, 1976

At 4:00 PM, a well-known W.O.R. interviewer named Jim Low arrived as expected. He brought a woman with him, and she carried a tape recorder. Little Edie allowed them into the dining room.

Doris arrived at the back door, and I let her in. We sat at the table to have coffee. Soon the phone rang. I knew by the way the shock waves went through me that it was Big Edie. She asked me to come up.

"Lois, ask Mr. Low if he would like something to drink, and give him some cookies. What are they doing down there? I don't want them in here today."

"Mr. Low is talking to Edie and his assistant has a tape recorder. I can't go in; Edie would be furious!"

"*Do it!* Take them some cookies now. Never mind Edie; go meet them!"

I went into the dining room, as Big Edie ordered, but left within seconds, as Edie certainly didn't like it.

Later, through Edie, Mr. Low and the woman went into Big Edie's room, and she talked with them. They didn't stay long, and shortly left.

Monday, April 5, 1976

I'm worried about my right eye. It looks odd. I made an appointment to see Dr. York tomorrow.

Heard on the radio tonight that Howard Hughes died! We talked about it, Little Edie said she had met him, and he asked her to go out with him, but she didn't care to.

Tuesday, April 6, 1976

I was listening to the "Fitzsgerard Program" when they were discussing the Blair Sabol write-up and the Beales.

This afternoon, Little Edie wanted to go to Guild Hall to vote. We at Grey Gardens are all for Jimmy Carter. However, Edie didn't go.

Wednesday, April 7, 1976

I talked with Doris on the telephone this morning after the Beales finished their conversation with her. She will be here tonight to listen with us to *The Jim Low Music Show* on W.O.R. It was a good Beale interview that he taped on April 3rd.

Sunday, April 11, 1976

Susan Froemke arrived today. She came into the kitchen-studio. The Beales knew she was there, but didn't see her, and soon she left, after looking at my paintings.

About five minutes after Susan departed, a knock on the front door, and I opened it. A man was standing there. "I'm with the U.P.I. Are you related to the Beales?"

"I'll tell Edie you are here. Wait a minute."

"Are *you* related to the Beales?"

I didn't answer him, and went upstairs to find Little Edie. She didn't want to talk with U.P.I. now. "Tell him to phone first, Lois."

When I returned downstairs, he was not in sight!

Friday, April 16, 1976

GOOD FRIDAY

We exchanged Easter cards.

This morning, while I happened to be looking out the kitchen-studio back window, a car stopped on Lily Pond Lane, by our black plastic trash bags. Little Edie and I had recently brought them to the "pick up spot." Much to my surprise, a woman jumped from the car, camera in hand. She photographed the trash bags quickly, and before I could get out the door, she had driven off! What a strange thing to be doing on Good Friday!

Sunday, April 18, 1976

EASTER SUNDAY

We had record-breaking heat this Sunday, 96 degrees at 2:00 PM. The 1896 record was broken.

With the windows closed, Grey Gardens seems cool, for some unknown reason.

We spent a quiet, spiritual time, aware of Christ in our lives.

Monday, April 19, 1976

Doris phoned again today, but she was upset, and needed to talk with Big Edie. A very fine friend of hers had died, a detective in Connecticut named Peter Petty. He was high ranking in his field.

Could Doris be somehow connected with investigations? She always carries a large handbag, and she phones or stops by every day. Why? Little Edie and I were always curious about Doris.

On Tuesday, Doris arrived, and wanted to show me what Peter Petty had once given her. She brought out of her bag a silver police whistle and looked at it with sad eyes.

Thursday, April 22, 1976

The celebration action continues. Some Rutgers University students connected with the college magazine arrived, and spent a lot of time at Grey Gardens. Little Edie liked them, much photography going on. Doris arrived. She wanted to be involved or watch everything that happens here. The Rutgers students even came into the kitchen-studio and photographed my paintings and took pictures of me. First time, I wondered why Edie brought them in. Their camera looked expensive. They promised to send us prints, but they never did. I wanted to see the photos of my paintings… Oh, well. Their recorder didn't stop going once, that I know of.

According to the ad in *The New York Times*: "*Grey Gardens:* last three days." Little Edie is slightly depressed about it, money being the reason.

Friday, April 23, 1976

David Maysles telephoned. He expects to be here tomorrow with his baby. Judy is fine. Other news; one of the Rutgers University men telephoned. They had been into see the Maysles and Susan Froemke.

The kitchen sink is not working right.

Saturday, April 24, 1976

About 10:45 AM, Mary Hedges called, wanting directions to the Beale house because some friends wanted their palms analyzed. I told Big and Little Edie and they were glad of it, as we are low on cash.

David and Judy phoned and said they couldn't visit today after all.

At 1:00 PM, Mary Hedges, two women, and a man arrived. The man, Larry, is half-owner of the house where I read palms in Wainscott. The lovely place on the ocean. I read all their hands, and it was pleasant, and money earned. The group left.

Later, one of the women phoned and asked me to read palms tomorrow at 11:00 AM.

Sunday, April 25, 1976

Pinky, Little Edie's favorite male cat that had sired the pink kittens, Pinky One and Pinky Two, is very ill. Edie busy talking to vets on the phone.

At 11:00 AM, the woman that called yesterday arrived with a couple, and I started to read their palms. While I was busy working, David Maysles telephoned. Great upset about the grocery bill. The Beales can't pay it, and wanted some money from David to assist them with the debt.

"No money now," said David. We were to continue to hear this for a long time.

My clients drove off after their readings in the kitchen-studio. I gave Little Edie two dollars from the ten.

Cloudy this morning, and then pouring rain. Coming out of the downpour, and onto the front porch, there appeared a veterinarian from Southampton! On a Sunday! Now I knew Pinky's illness was critical. Edie carried the cat downstairs and opened the heavy door.

"Oh, come in," she whispered as I went through the dining room.

The vet administered to poor Pinky. He didn't stay long.

Monday, April 26, 1976

CONFEDERATE MEMORIAL DAY

I felt sorry for Little Edie and Big Edie because of Pinky's death today. Edie placed the body in a box, and brought it from their bedroom to the back porch. She intended to have a funeral later, and closed the box so the raccoons wouldn't see the body. Brooks expected to dig a grave tomorrow, then a short service, and burial.

Soon Little Edie changed the subject, and we talked of the Civil War. Edie's great-grandfather, on the Beale side, John Phelan, swore in Jefferson Davis, President of the Confederacy. Judge Phelan certainly helped start the Civil War.

Edie intends to go into New York tomorrow, and it has nothing to do with the Maysles. I was shocked. Edie received an invitation to an important ballet opening, and a party. Since the Maysles were not involved, Edie would have to pay her own way, and no Deanna to assist us here. I couldn't believe it. But, Edie telephoned the Martha Washington Hotel and made reservations for Tuesday night. The filmmakers were not to be informed.

Tonight, I wondered how Pinky could have a funeral.

Doris is going to stay at Grey Gardens while Edie is away. She seems to want her to attend the party. There has evidently been much conversation about it.

The Maysles want Edie to attend an opening of her film in Boston May 5th, and I don't think she wants to go.

I wondered about the trip to New York City, if this time Little Edie might not come back to East Hampton as expected. After all, without the Maysles, Edie on her own, who could be certain?

Big Edie seemed almost indifferent… perhaps she knew something I didn't. No doubt, she did.

Tuesday, April 27, 1976

At 6:30 AM, I spoke with Little Edie about Pinky. "You can't just go away and leave your dead cat in a box on the porch. Nothing happened to the box last night, but the raccoons haven't discovered the body yet. I did notice some of your other males keeping a vigil this morning."

"Oh, Whiskers… He fought with Pinky… and he's glad he's dead. Black Cat would like to know what happened to him, and so would I. Do you think the vet gave him a shot to speed his death? I guess he did, all the other cats ran and hid when he came. Did you notice?"

"You should have Pinky's funeral today, you shouldn't neglect him, his spirit will be angry. It's more important than the ballet and a party!"

"No! I'm going and nothing can stop me! I'm going to put the box inside the servants' toilet room that's on the back porch. Brooks uses it when he's here, except he couldn't get in there when he was too drunk when I went away for three days because it was locked and I couldn't find the key. I'm sorry he had to use your bathroom, Lois. God! I finally found the key!"

"It's not right! The body will start to smell!"

"It will not! The porch is in the shade. Don't worry about my Pinky!"

The phone rang. "It's Mother! Tell her I'll be up in a minute." Edie went out to move the cardboard coffin.

Doris appeared at 7:15 AM, and at 7:30, Edie left on the small jitney-bus for New York. The jitney stopped in front of the house for her, as requested.

Brooks arrived at 10:00 AM. He asked Big Edie if she wanted him to bury Pinky, having noticed the body in the toilet room. Edie had left the door unlocked.

Big Edie only said, "We don't want Pinky buried today, Brooks, but work outside on the grounds."

Little Edie received $100 check from the Maysles; I had driven into town for the mail. Big Edie opened the envelope hoping for some money.

Doris was extremely busy all day long. She left for an hour to check on her poodle while Big Edie waited for her return, exhibiting impatience. Something could happen to her once out of the boundary of Grey Gardens.

Brooks left this afternoon.

I cooked dinner for all, as Doris had brought chopped steak, and we ate in our usual places.

Many ill kittens in Big Edie's bedroom, and Doris discovered that one large kitten, another pink, had died. She placed it in an attractive box she found.

We retired about 10:00 PM. Doris had her monk's robe on again. Little Edie never telephoned.

Big Edie told Doris that she could open the window slightly by Little Edie's bed, which was the bed on which Doris slept.

Wednesday, April 28, 1976

Everyone was up before 7:00 AM. Big Edie was in the porch room where Doris had rolled her. They were getting air and sunlight, and selected cats were with them. Others, for some reason known only to Big Edie, had to be restricted to other areas inside the house. This is not an easy job, as Doris had to locate each and every feline. They had already been fed.

Big Edie told me that when there were many new kittens, Little Edie's disposition was *much* better, and she smiled thinking about it.

Doris had to leave again to check on her poodle. I phoned The Martha Washington Hotel, but Edie had checked out. Doris returned.

At 11:30 AM, Big Edie asked me to drive to the East Hampton railroad station. I did, and Little Edie got off the train. We checked the mail and drove home.

Edie didn't see the ballet; the trip wasn't worth all the trouble. When she writes her autobiography at age 90, she said, perhaps we will know what happened April 27th, 1976.

Doris had coffee with me while mother and daughter talked. Doris left Grey Gardens exhausted, saying "the cats are too much!" and that she couldn't sleep because of the lack of fresh air.

Little Edie seemed changed, and I wouldn't say for the best. She appeared disturbed, I thought.

Edie telephoned David to tell him that she can't fly to Boston for the film opening. He didn't know Edie was in New York, and was amazed. Edie told him that many photographers were taking her picture at a nightclub.

Later, Susan Froemke telephoned, and explained that the Maysles want Edie in Boston.

Pinky has still not been buried.

Thursday, April 29, 1976

Last night, Susan Froemke phoned Doris to ask her if she would stay with Big Edie while Edie flew to Boston, and Doris said she would. Deanna Douglas is unavailable now.

I could see this morning that Little Edie is too tired to go to Boston, and Big Edie says it's too far.

The Maysles are most upset, as they say that "it's a commitment for publicity." The film will open in Boston on May 5th.

Little Edie met me in the upstairs hall. "Oh, Lois, if I'm in Boston, I'll get involved with the school bussing issue and be *killed*! The parents there are enraged."

"I know…"

"I can't go."

"Edie, I think you should have Pinky's funeral today. Brooks is here, and can dig the grave now. This is the fourth day since his death! The kitten should be buried, too."

"No. I'm too tired to select the proper site. I loved Pinky, and it's important."

Doris stopped by.

Friday, April 30, 1976

There are too many kittens here, and they keep the Beales too busy!

Ever since Little Edie returned from New York, she has been most upset about fire and burglary. She was so frightened about them that she didn't even want me to have lunch downstairs in the kitchen-studio. She said she needed me upstairs where I can watch for burglars. I wouldn't do it.

This morning, Brooks and Edie buried Pinky. At long last! Edie was very emotional. Big Edie was frantic about having all the kittens in her room while the funeral service went on outside. They were falling off the bed.

May 1976

Saturday, May 1, 1976

It was cloudy this morning, and then there was a rainstorm. Every one in here is in an odd humor. Perhaps I will leave soon. There seems to be a change. The house wants something.

A woman telephoned for a hand reading, just one person. She says she knows the Maysles.

At 5:15 PM, the woman arrived as expected. Doris appeared first, and went upstairs to Big Edie's room. The woman was here quite a while, and seemed impressed with my analysis of her hands. The woman gave me no information about herself, and left. She looked like some kind of a "judge type."

I went out to dinner at Ma Berman's, now Nick & Toni's, with Doris.

Sunday, May 2, 1976

Doris stopped by again. She had luncheon with her mother-in-law, Mrs. Don Francisco Sr., at the Maidstone Club. She said they mentioned my cousin, Jane Erdmann, or Mrs. Morgan Whitney. Jane is a member of the club.

Monday, May 3, 1976

Doris arrived unexpectedly. I was delighted to see her. She talked with Big Edie and then came down into the kitchen-studio for a cup of coffee. She said to call her tomorrow.

The press release from *The Boston Globe* gave *Grey Gardens* a very good write-up.

Wednesday, May 5, 1976

Little Edie seems quiet, and Big Edie seems preoccupied. They talk about Phelan Beale, Little Edie's favorite brother, who lives in Oklahoma. He recently retired.

A large ad in today's *New York Times*, *Grey Gardens* is now playing in three theaters: one in Manhasset on Long Island; The New Yorker, and The 8th Street Playhouse in the Village. The Beales still have not received any money from the Maysles. It's sad. Once, when we were all sitting in the bedroom, David had asked Big Edie, "What are you going to do with all the money from the movie?"

"Why, I'm going to buy a piano," she answered.

Little Edie looked interested. "We need a car, Mother, after all the bills are paid!"

The Beales started to really enjoy the conversation. However, I thought David appeared uncomfortable, and he changed the subject.

Today's *Daily News* gave us a shock! In large, bold print at the top of Suzy's column, it stated, "The CAPRICIOUS RICHIE BERLIN will spend her summer at Grey Gardens!"

Little Edie said she didn't know a thing about it, but that she wouldn't allow her on the property. The Beales didn't know her, but she might have met her mother, Mrs.

Richard Berlin. Mr. Berlin was chairman of the board of the Hearst Corporation for 44 years.

There had never been a phone call from the "capricious" Miss Berlin.

Doris read the column today, and couldn't understand it. We talked and laughed about it, but for some time, Little Edie and I watched the cars that slowed down in front of the house. We wondered when a long black limousine would drive in, and a woman would step out, followed by loads of luggage!

We all watched *The Daily News* for information, but nothing more ever showed up.

Aware of the Patty Hearst kidnapping, we were worried that someone would think Miss Berlin lives here and try to break in and seize her for ransom. Perhaps underground members of the SLA or some other group would try something. They could kidnap Little Edie or me by mistake!

This article by *The Daily News* was worse than their $50,000 Onassis clothes mistake months earlier.

"God! What next?!" Little Edie said. "Be very careful going in and out."

"It's terrible to be kidnapped!"

"Watch for cars following you on Lily Pond Lane, Lois."

"What about reading palms in the kitchen-studio?"

"Oh, that's all right, you know who your clients are, and Mother talks to them on the telephone first."

I did continue to feel uncomfortable when I walked to West End Road for the newspaper and the cars going alone slowed. Before this bombshell in *The Daily News*, I knew they were only *Grey Gardens* fans or tourists.

"Now, Lois, if anyone snatches you for Richie Berlin, we can't pay any ransom." Little Edie smiled.

Sunday, May 9, 1976

MOTHER'S DAY

I gave Big Edie a card and two gifts. She told me she expected a Mother's Day card. We had an argument about it, so I made one.

Doris stopped by, and then we all had ice cream in Big Edie's room.

Tuesday, May 11, 1976

Doris called early this morning. She talked with Big Edie and said she saw her niece, Jacqueline, on TV last night, and thought she looked thin.

Doris phones and then stops by *every* day. She also asked me to phone her every day, after she talks with the Beales in the morning.

Big Edie seems to understand all this, but Little Edie and I do not. It must be that Doris loves Big Edie, as she has often said, and Big Edie enjoys it, and loves her.

Tuesday, May 18, 1976

Brooks is here working, and he certainly is perfect now, no drinking and feels well.

Doris arrived with a new lampshade that Big Edie needed from "the ten-cent store."

Doris said she liked the portrait I had painted of my mother a long time ago. I had just finished painting the frame another color.

Wednesday, May 19, 1976

JOHN VERNOU BOUVIER III's BIRTHDAY

Pouring rain and strong winds. It's "Black Jack" Bouvier's birthday again, and we mentioned the date.

"This year, there will be no flowers on Jack's grave, so you don't have to go to the cemetery, Lois," Big Edie said.

"Why not? Jacqueline didn't order any for her father this year?"

"She wouldn't."

"Why not?"

"Because of our movie."

"Oh," I answered.

The house is chilly as the oil burner went off this morning, just after Schenck delivered oil, but by afternoon, the heating system was working again.

Much phone ringing tonight, but I went to sleep at 10:30 PM, as usual. Outside of "Ma Bell," the house is quiet.

Only a small amount of palm reading goes on.

Saturday, May 22, 1976

It is a peaceful Saturday in Grey Gardens. Doris arrived, and Big Edie said, "She arrives every day."

Monday, May 24, 1976

This afternoon and evening, I painted a spirit portrait of Doris as I noticed her on the front porch in a past reincarnation. I told her about it at the time of the happening. I had to explain, as I had such a surprised expression. She changed from Doris into this other woman of a past age in history and then back into Doris.

Thursday, May 27, 1976

Doris arrived early this afternoon. She had seen the strange portrait last Tuesday and seemed impressed. The Beales were interested, too.

At 4:00 PM, while Doris was sitting in Big Edie's room, two clients for palm reading arrived, a young woman and a man. They were friends of Mr. Ackerman, an attorney in East Hampton. Everyone enjoyed the hand analysis, and then they left the kitchen-studio.

Doris came down and had coffee with me.

Saturday, May 29, 1976

The David Maysles are expected here today: David, Judy, and their baby, John Phillip.

As usual, Doris telephoned, and suggested that she and I drive to a dress shop in Sag Harbor. We left about 1:30 PM and looked in other stores in addition to the dress shop. At long last, we returned to Grey Gardens. I thought the Maysles would have been there and left, however, they had not even arrived. Shortly, they drove into the grounds.

Doris wanted to show them the two portraits I had painted, one of Little Edie and one of herself, but David's attention went to the portrait of my mother, and the past life portrait of Doris. Later, Little Edie showed David the painting of Cap Krug.

When we returned upstairs, I took some photographs at Big Edie's request. She was holding John Phillip on her lap.

The Beales with John Phillip

As it was strictly a social visit, the Beales couldn't mention money as they had planned... not with a new baby they hadn't met before.

Monday, May 31, 1976

MEMORIAL DAY

Doris on the phone said she might stop by later. At 4:00 PM, I put my black bathing suit on for the first time this year and went outside by the back porch to read. Since I couldn't lock the door after myself, and Edie was busy, and I wanted to be free to go in and out of the house, I had to sit in a certain location, as a guard would, to keep my eyes on the door. The Beales insisted on this. The ocean beach was very close, but I could never go, as it was too complicated.

Another quiet day... and no one kidnapped.

June 1976

Tuesday, June 1, 1976

Big Edie was on the telephone all morning. She wanted to talk with her son Buddy about the grocery bill. Later, she talked with Doris and others. Big Edie had conversed with David Maysles, since he had been here, about paying something on the food bill.

A postal from Susan Froemke from Cannes. She wrote that "the film is a sensation, with French subtitles."

I started another painting, a face, but didn't know who it would turn out to be.

Wednesday, June 2, 1976

I finished the painting and showed it to the Beales.

"Why, it's my brother Jack!" Big Edie looked intently at me.

I didn't know who it was, so I had written on it, "The Great Actor."

"It's 'Black Jack' all right!" Little Edie said.

Big Edie spoke again, "Lois, make the jawbone larger; Jacqueline gets her large jawbone from her father."

Thursday, June 3, 1976

Doris is here. She seems very interested in Frank Sinatra. Knew him once quite well, she said. She seems to have known every celebrity except Lee Radziwill. Of course, Jacqueline is above the level of celebrity.

Tuesday, June 8, 1976

Little Edie is busy getting ready to go to Southampton to see her doctor for a checkup. So, I left for town and returned.

About 1:00 PM, Doris arrived. She had dropped Peter off at the playground. Jack Helmuth couldn't drive Edie as he is not feeling well, and Big Edie wanted me to remain here. A cab arrived for Edie, and she left for the bus stop.

Doris was in Big Edie's bedroom all afternoon. They called the Maysles, and Doris talked with David about the large grocery bill. David said he would phone The Newtown Store to ask them to extend the Beales additional credit.

Little Edie phoned from Southampton to tell us she would arrive on the six-something bus. I met Edie in town and drove her home. So far, she has never been in Doris's car.

Edie had a complete examination. The doctor was concerned about her neck, and sent her to another doctor. He wanted her to go to the Southampton Hospital for more tests. She refused, and that ended that. Little Edie thought the doctor might think the worst, and bring out the knife.

Thursday, June 10, 1976

The Beales' grocery bill problems continue. Big Edie talked to one or both of the Maysles this morning. They are going to California tomorrow and will do nothing about the bill. They will return in two weeks. Big Edie looked sad.

Saturday, June 12, 1976

This afternoon, I attended the Daughters of the American Revolution meeting at The Maidstone Club. When I returned, I found Little Edie furious that I had been talking to Maidstone Club people. I told her it wasn't my fault that the D.A.R. held their meeting there. Big Edie didn't appreciate my going. I hadn't realized they would be so upset.

Tuesday, June 15, 1976

I met Vinson Hayes today. He wants me to paint two murals on heavy art paper for the Beaux Arts Ball by Saturday. They will be about five feet long and two feet wide. I agreed to do it, as I would be paid 40 dollars for them.

Wednesday, June 16, 1976

Little Edie said not to paint the murals here. I didn't say anything, but decided to paint them, as I could work at night in the kitchen-studio. By Thursday evening, the murals were finished, and I let the Beales see them. Little Edie didn't seem too displeased. I think she wanted the one of George Washington.

Friday, June 18, 1976

Doris Francisco's Birthday

The Beales are getting ready for Doris's birthday event. Little Edie cleaned the top of the round metal table in the upstairs hall where we would all be gathered. Big Edie ordered cake and ice cream from the Newtown. Their credit had been further extended, making the grocery bill higher and higher. But it couldn't be helped, and would be paid "when the movie money" came in.

Doris arrived, and the Beales were waiting for her in the hall. "Here's the birthday girl," Big Edie said, and then sang "Happy Birthday to you, Doris" in good voice. She still sang every morning for a while. I could hear her on my way downstairs for breakfast.

This was the last time Big Edie would sing Happy Birthday to anyone, but we didn't know it then.

Big Edie cut the cake, passed it around, dished the ice cream, and was entertaining and charming.

We gave Doris her wrapped presents.

It was a clear, hot day. Later, Doris left, and Big Edie sang to her as she went down the wide front stairs. I know she enjoyed the party; we all did.

Tuesday, June 22, 1976

Still no word from Miss Berlin. Very odd.

The weather is getting quite warm now, and soon the "dreaded fleas" will attack Grey Gardens and everything living in it. I wonder how the "capricious Richie Berlin" will cope, if she ever gets here. The Beales have stopped thinking about it.

Wednesday, June 23, 1976

On June 25th, I am going to leave. I have been living in this unique house for thirteen months. I have been very close to Big and Little Edie, but it's time to go away… not far, however. I am going to stay with Doris Francisco.

Thursday, June 24, 1976

I have this feeling that a strong current, a stream of consciousness that runs through the house is moving me swiftly and gently from the Eye Room, as if it were doing me a favor. I did wonder how the Beales would get along. I knew the terrible answer within to weeks. This was my last night at Grey Gardens until February 1977.

As I packed yesterday and today, I realized a couple of ghosts-spirits were leaving with me, and I was glad of it.

Brooks arrived, and Doris stopped by. She went upstairs to confer with Big Edie while I continued to work. Doris didn't stay too long.

I was removing paintings from the kitchen-studio walls when Little Edie came in.

"Lois, will you leave The Cross painting for me?" She smiled and pointed at the large Masonite over the coal stove.

"But Edie! That's my chapel!"

"You don't have room for it at Doris's."

"Yes, I do. I'm storing all my paintings in her basement. Doris said I could. I haven't been in her house, as you know, but she told me there's loads of space!"

Little Edie frowned. "What will you sell it for? I'll give you $100 when I get some money."

I felt a sudden sadness for Edie and said, "I'll leave the painting here. It's really not for sale. Well, you can pay me someday. By the way, some ghosts are going with me."

"I don't care! Cap isn't!"

"No, he isn't."

Edie glided smoothly to the door, scraped it open, and went back upstairs to give her mother a chocolate milk.

By evening, I was tired from all the packing. After a light dinner, I said good night to the Beales, and walked towards my room. Black Cat, lying on the stairway railing, gazed steadily at me. I hesitated, and stared back at him.

I went to sleep so quickly on my stretcher-cot. The last mental image I have of Grey Gardens is Black Cat's eyes. They were, and still are, enormous in my mind's eye.

Friday, June 25, 1976

It was a clear day. Brooks arrived and helped me carry luggage, paintings, and things down the back stairs. Of course, Doris telephoned.

I went in the bedroom to see Big Edie. She wanted me to leave the two beach ocean scenes I had painted.

"They look just like Uncle Edgar's work, Lois."

We had often talked about his life.

"Will you and Edie hang them in the porch room before you go? I want them on the pink wall, across from Uncle Edgar's painting."

Once again, I felt an intense sadness that lasted for a brief moment, or perhaps an eternity, who would know in Grey Gardens, except Big Edie.

I hung the two painting where they belonged.

The Beales were pleased and I was, too.

Early this afternoon, the Home Sweet Home Movers arrived and soon my things were arranged in the van. I got into the Ghia and followed the truck to No. One, Duke Drive.

After the unloading, I telephoned the Beales to tell them that it went along well.

July 1976

Friday, July 2, 1976

I found it pleasant living at Doris's house. She wanted me to go to the beach with her every day, and I did. We didn't stop by to see Big and Little Edie, just talked on the telephone every morning. Doris believed that I needed fresh air and sun and also a rest from my long visit at Grey Gardens. I really enjoyed the cool, refreshing water on my body, and wondered if Little Edie would ever get in the ocean this summer.

Doris and I heard that their film would start playing at The Old Post Office Cinema in East Hampton on July 14th. I hoped the Beales would be able to attend the local premiere, that somehow it would be possible for them. But, I had a strange feeling, as if something might be wrong at the old mansion. However, the Beales sounded fine on the telephone...

Tuesday, July 6, 1976

This date in 1976 started the beginning of the end for Edith Bouvier Beale, but Doris and I didn't know that. We had our usual morning chat.

A clear sky, warm weather, we left for the beach.

Wednesday, July 7, 1976

Cloudy and humid. At 11:00 AM, Doris dialed the familiar number, 324-0343, and Little Edie answered. Doris could hear Big Edie in the background, but she sounded a long way off, and weak. We finally found out that Big Edie had fallen from the rolling chair and been on the floor all night, lying on the cat papers under a dressing table by the bedroom floor. Little Edie had telephoned the local police, and the officers had placed Big Edie on her bed, somehow. It took quite a while. Dr. Rowe arrived, but Little Edie refused to allow him to see her mother. Also, she didn't want us to drive over.

I thought Big Edie might have a broken leg. Whatever happened to her, she never really recovered. Grey Gardens started to deteriorate. The house wasn't well. It seemed upset. Old houses have feelings.

Thursday, July 8, 1976

I talked with the Beales early this morning. Big Edie still sounded weak, but closer to the phone. Little Edie said her Mother needed a prescription from the drug store, a pain killer that Dr. Rowe ordered.

During the course of conversation, I found out that Brooks helped the police officers move Big Edie from the floor to the bed. He wasn't there when the accident happened, only Little Edie. For reasons known only to the Beales, Big Edie had tumbled with unusual force from the rolling chair that had belonged to my mother. I was puzzled, as I certainly knew it to be quite safe, and Big Edie had used it for well over a year without trouble.

Little Edie asked Doris to pick up the prescription. Before we left Duke Drive, Doris found an insulated bag that had been used in Connecticut on a yacht, and packed with ice. Of course, the Beales didn't have any. Doris also got a few clean small towels and washcloths.

We left right away for White's Drug Store, and then arrived at Grey Gardens.

Big Edie didn't want anyone to touch her or look at her legs except Doris. She didn't want Little Edie to administer to the swelling and huge bruises in any way.

Doris gently placed ice packs on the injured area. Big Edie's face appeared quite pale, or grey in color. We strongly suggested a doctor from The Medical Group, but the thin woman in bed said, "No, I don't feel well enough to have a doctor right now. Perhaps in a few days."

I was frightened that Big Edie might have a fractured leg. She couldn't move without great pain. Little Edie was standing in the room, quietly, with her arms folded, like a sentinel on guard.

There was nothing more Doris and I could do. We left Grey Gardens depressed. I noticed the cats seemed different. They were aware of what had transpired within the old house.

Friday, July 9, 1976

My Birthday

My first thoughts when I woke up this morning were centered on Big Edie. She must be suffering with pain, and she couldn't go to the porch room. She would have to remain in the same position as we had left her. It was horrible to think about.

I don't even feel like it's my birthday. For the first time in many years, I will not hear Big Edie's lovely voice singing, "Happy Birthday, Dear Lois."

Doris had talked with Little Edie on the telephone, and we had to dress to leave for Grey Gardens.

Big Edie told her daughter she wanted to speak with Doris and me separately and alone. However, Little Edie didn't leave her Mother's room longer than a few minutes.

Mrs. Don Francisco inspected the bruises again, and tried to arrange Big Edie's head in a more comfortable position. She had also brought ice to place in the towels.

Later, Doris and I walked out into the hot, butterfly day. Here, it would be fleas, and not butterflies!

You could hear the ocean, and smell the sea and the thick honeysuckle, the wild roses, and the tall hedges in bloom.

Two women, now confined as prisoners in the house that dominated them, owned them, would not enjoy the beautiful grounds, and clear delightful air. I knew Little Edie wouldn't leave her mother to go out on the upstairs porch. She would stay in the bedroom. I believed that Big Edie should go to the Southampton Hospital, as Dr. Rowe wanted. If she didn't, only a dark grave would receive her.

I felt a change in the house. It had the regretful, sorrowful expression that some abandoned houses have, not haunted, just lonely and tragic.

The Beales did not ask me to return, to live there again. Their pride wouldn't permit it. I would have to offer.

Every day, Doris and I drove to and from Grey Gardens.

Of course, I phoned Dr. Rowe at The Medical Group, shortly after Big Edie's accident, but he told me that he couldn't examine Mrs. Beale without her permission, so no doctor ever entered Big Edie's bedroom.

It was a difficult situation in which to intercede as both Beales could use their telephones to summon help any time they wanted. Some kind of fear seemed to keep them from the necessary assistance that Big Edie needed.

Doris could only try to make Big Edie comfortable, and without Doris, I don't think she could have lived through the summer. She still would not have gone to the hospital, or had a doctor, and would have suffered additional anguish of body and mind. She wanted Doris with her as much as possible.

Big Edie didn't really need me in the warm, flea-infested bedroom, so many of the days I just sat in the car until Doris came out the door. She always looked grim as she approached me, but I knew she had been smiling and gentle with Big Edie. Doris was covered with fleas, and I would brush them off her back and shoulders while she flicked them off her front and around her ankles. After Doris wiped her hands with an alcohol-damp paper cloth, we drove off the grounds.

Wednesday, July 14, 1976

The movie *Grey Gardens* opens tonight! Early this afternoon, Doris and I drove to the Beales. Little Edie opened the back door and we went inside. I stayed in the kitchen talking with Edie while Doris administered to Big Edie.

The kitchen didn't look inviting with the two chairs and table moved against the wall. I noticed another hole in the ceiling near the light fixture. However, the Silver Cross painting was still over the old coal stove. The small gas stove wasn't being used at all. There was nothing else in the room. It was empty.

I gave Edie a movie poster, a colored photo of her standing in front of Grey Gardens. She will not be able to attend. Big Edie is still in pain, and can't move her legs at all. It is impossible for her to leave the bed. I feel so very sorry for her, but what I can I do? Doris came downstairs and we left.

Doris talked with Father Huntington and Father Joe recently, as she upset about Big Edie's condition.

Doris, her son Peter, and I arrived at the 8:45 PM showing of the film. I couldn't help but feel depressed and Doris was crying softly at the end of the movie. We felt worse than anyone in the theater, knowing how Big Edie was suffering and so very few people aware of it. Nothing like the last time we saw the movie in New York City, while the main star of the film enjoyed her view of the overgrown gardens and vivid blue slice of ocean in the distance. I recalled how Big Edie turned to Doris before we left and said, "Why don't you change your mind and stay, Babes? It's so lovely on the outside porch now."

Remember? Now she can't go there, and the vines are thick over the bedroom windows.

Doris, Peter, and I left the Old Post Office Cinema quietly.

Thursday, July 15, 1976

I talked to Little Edie on the front lawn today while Doris remained with Big Edie. I wanted her to telephone Dr. Rowe or someone at The Medical Group.

"Lois, I can't! Mother will not allow me to."

"I would phone anyway."

"I can't! She would hear me, and cancel the doctor."

"Then call when your mother is sleeping."

"God! If she went to the hospital, they would cut off her legs or operate on her somewhere and kill her!"

"They would not!"

"Lois Wright! You put your mother in the hospital and she died! She wanted to leave! She asked for a lawyer to get out of the Southampton Hospital. I know *all* about it!"

"You do not!"

"Your mother *died* there."

"What about another hospital, one in New York?"

"My mother isn't going unless she wants to, kiddo. She's a Bouvier, and it's her life and she's in charge of it! I told her she could go to the hospital any time she wanted, but I wouldn't go to her funeral if she did."

Doris opened the door and came outside. Little Edie said goodbye and slipped quickly into the house.

After returning to Duke Drive, and hearing about Big Edie's condition, I telephoned her son Bouvier at his office in New York City.

I told him his mother had fallen from her rolling chair on July 6th, an accident.

Bouvier sounded upset. He had known nothing about the matter. Bouvier said he "would find out about it." I hope he will be able to get a doctor for Big Edie. However, I doubted that he could, so I decided to write Jacqueline a note. After all, she is sending small checks every month. She is interested in her aunt's life or she wouldn't be helping her. I knew Little Edie would be angry, but I mailed the sad information to 1040 Fifth, certified. I wondered if Jacqueline could send a doctor to Grey Gardens. I didn't ask her to. My hope was that Big Edie would have a doctor if her favorite niece strongly suggested it.

Friday, July 16, 1976

Big Edie's condition is worse. Doris and I arrived at Grey Gardens as usual. It started to rain very hard. I sat in the car, waiting.

On our way back, on Lily Pond Lane, Doris said she did all that she could for Big Edie, but she still can't move in bed and has a terrible open bed sore on her lower back. Doris is trying to keep it clean. A difficult job with the cats. It's impossible.

Doris phoned David Maysles this evening and talked with him.

Saturday, July 16, 1976

Doris and I attended the late showing of *Grey Gardens* at the Old Post Office Cinema. It was "meet the filmmakers" night. David said he would be there to answer questions from the audience after the film ended. We met David in the lobby and also the woman mentioned in Suzy's column in The Daily News. The famous Richie Berlin who had intended to "spend the summer at Grey Gardens." She told us that she had seen the movie thirteen times and wanted to tape it tonight. After the questions and answers, Ms. Berlin kissed Doris and gave her an expensive silver fish necklace. She placed it on her as if it were a medal. Doris only smiled and said, "Thank you." I wondered just what prompted Ms. Berlin to give Doris the necklace. They had never met, and didn't know each other. Or did they? Doris loves anything with a fish design. Doris Francisco wasn't in the movie, and should have been a total stranger to Richie. I thought it odd, but no one explained it to me.

Ms. Berlin's next move was more reasonable, but still unusual. She asked me to give Little Edie a link belt made with the heavy Berlin silver. Forks with a B on them. I heard later that it's worth around $700, or so Richie said. Little Edie would appreciate it. After that, Doris and I left. David said he didn't know Ms. Berlin.

Sunday, July 18, 1976

There is a write-up in today's *New York Times* about the movie. Doris and I drove to Grey Gardens later this afternoon. First, Doris wanted to stop at the Sea Spray Inn in East Hampton and see Richie. We sat outside with Richie at a table. Ms. Berlin produced her autograph book again. Last night she had asked Doris and me to write something in it. She hoped that Little Edie would sign it also when I gave her the Berlin belt.

Later, Little Edie accepted the gift casually, standing by the sink in the kitchen. She wrote in Richie's book at my request, and that seemed to end the episode. I think Edie talked on the phone once with Richie during the long, difficult summer. Doris wore the silver fish.

Tuesday, July 20, 1976

This morning, Nancy Tuckerman telephoned from New York and asked for me. She said that Jackie left for Russia last night, so she asked her to call. Nancy had given Jacqueline some letters to read on the way to the airport in the car. After her arrival and just before the flight time, she phoned from the airport, as she was quite concerned about her aunt.

Shortly, I put Doris on the phone to give Nancy the details regarding Big Edie's condition.

This afternoon, Doris and I drove to Grey Gardens, but didn't mention the telephone call.

Friday, July 23, 1976

I mailed a note to Nancy Tuckerman and Jacqueline this morning.

Tuesday, July 27, 1976

This is the last night for the Maysles film to play at the small theater on Newtown Lane. Doris and I went to see it once more. On our way out, a woman stopped us and asked for an on-the-spot interview. She had talked with Little Edie today, and explained that she is a writer for *Newsday*, Carol Agus.

Friday, July 30, 1976

Today is the Ladies Village Improvement Society Fair Day. The Beales were always interested in it and liked to go. I have a photograph of Big Edie and Little Edie and me, standing near the palmistry tents with our Fortune Committee ribbon on. It was taken in the early '60s by a New York photographer for the Social Spectator magazine, and Big Edie had many copies made. She gave me one or two. I didn't read palms there.

Doris and I went to the fair, bought gifts for the Beales, and then arrived at Grey Gardens. I sat in the bedroom for a while and felt depressed. However, Big Edie's face didn't seem as pale, but her daughter lacked even a tiny bit of tan. She has been with her mother day and night since the accident, hardly leaving the upstairs of the old house. Big Edie's mind seemed as clear as ever, but she was still suffering and could only move an inch at a time with great effort in her bed.

Saturday, July 31, 1976

Doris told me today that Big Edie said Jacqueline phoned about her accident, asked her to have x-rays taken, and said that a doctor should examine her. Big Edie promised to see about it Monday or Tuesday. Jacqueline informed her that Nancy told her, but Big Edie didn't understand how Nancy found out.

AUGUST 1976

Monday, August 2, 1976

About 10:00 this morning, while Doris was on the phone with a friend I didn't know, she let her wonderful poodle out the back door. Within five minutes, he was dead, killed by a hit-and-run driver. Doris was so shocked and upset that I called the Beales right away. I thought Big Edie would be the only one that could comfort Doris, and she did.

Later, we stopped by Grey Gardens with their mail.

The *Newsday* write-up by Ms. Agus was in yesterday's paper. My quote sounded as if I didn't want Big Edie to go to the hospital, and I do.

Wednesday, August 4, 1976

This afternoon, while Little Edie was locking Doris and me out the back door, a strange woman appeared on the narrow porch, frightening everyone. The woman was also startled to see us. Edie dashed upstairs. The woman was Joyce Egginton of *The Observer*, London, England. She said that she is visiting in North Haven and that she has read the *Newsday* interview. We were pleasant to her. Ms. Egginton had telephoned Edie, but she wouldn't talk with her at all. We said we would give Edie her card.

Thursday, August 5, 1976

Parts of Big Edie's mind were agitated and disturbed. She believes that three nurses are in the room with her, and she wants Doris and me to tell them to leave. She thinks Little Edie is in New York.

We were at Grey Gardens almost two hours, while Doris calmed Big Edie.

Sunday, August 8, 1976

It is pouring rain and the start of a hurricane.

I wrote another note to report to Jacqueline and Nancy. I will mail it tomorrow.

Monday, August 9, 1976

I am worried about the Beales. All day, it is on the radio that we will be hit by Hurricane Belle around 5:00 PM. The heavy rain from yesterday continues today. There are many phone called back and forth from Grey Gardens. Later, Doris, Peter, and I drove into town. It was busy with people buying flashlights and candles, men and women running from their cars with shorts on and colored rain slickers. I mailed the envelope to 1040 Fifth, carrying it into the post office in a paper bag so it wouldn't get soaked.

We arrived at Grey Gardens and had to park outside on West End Road. Doris went upstairs with ice cream. Little Edie said her Mother wanted to see me, but I had to sit in the car with Peter. Her mind had cleared, however, Doris said she would not allow Peter to remain in the car alone, and she couldn't take him into the house today. Peter was difficult. I never knew what Big Edie wanted to tell me on August 9th.

Doris, Peter, and I drove back to Duke Drive and turned the radio on again. The Beales had their Sony. They had been asked by the police department to evacuate. An officer had stopped by and Little Edie talked with him from the window. He said the Sea Spray Inn near Lily Pond Lane had been evacuated, and all along the waterfronts. Only the Beales were left. The officer had made a second attempt to talk to the two inhabitants of Grey Gardens into leaving, but they wouldn't.

Doris conversed with Richie on the phone. She had left the Sea Spray with other guests and was staying in Southampton with a friend, Marjorie Jenks. Monty Rock was also there, a TV nightclub star.

There were reports on the radio that indicated we would have winds from 75 to 125 miles an hour, and the storm would strike tonight.

Little Edie had her bathing suit on.

Tuesday, August 10, 1976

It was a frightful storm and our electric went off at 12:05 AM. By the morning, the hurricane winds were gone. The entire house runs on electricity (the water pump, the stove), so we have nothing except the telephone. The Beales are better off, as they have "city" water and they have a gas stove, but they can't use the hotplate.

Last night, we talked with Big and Little Edie on the phone until very late. The worst of the storm was at 2:30 AM. I could see the trees bending down to the ground in the yard, large trees, one fell. I didn't sleep until nearly dawn.

Doris worried about Big Edie and got up early. She left for town about 8:30 AM. She wanted to stop at the place under the bridge for coffee and rolls to take to the Beales and to check for damage. There wasn't any, but a shocking amount of large trees were uprooted in East Hampton, and some had fallen through the roofs of houses.

In the afternoon, we drove to Grey Gardens again to leave flashlights that Doris had managed to obtain. They were needed.

Thursday, August 12, 1976

The electric didn't work here until this evening!

One day this week, after the hurricane, Doris talked with Nancy Tuckerman on the telephone. She seemed pleased that Doris had called and said she would be having lunch with Jackie and would tell her all about her aunt's condition.

Thursday, August 19, 1976

At 11:00 PM, the phone rang. It was Big Edie on the line. She wanted us to drive over right away. She said Little Edie wouldn't help her, wouldn't get up, and wouldn't talk with her. Big Edie sounded frantic!

Doris, Peter, and I quickly left for Grey Gardens. Little Edie let us in. She said her mother had been complaining a great deal and was angry at her. Big Edie had lost track of time and would demand dinner at 3:00 AM, thinking it was 6:00 PM.

Peter went into Big Edie's bedroom for the first time and sat down. We remained until Big Edie was able to go to sleep, and then left.

Friday, August 20, 1976

Of course, we were at Grey Gardens today. Quite often during the month of August, Doris would stop at White's Drug Store and buy items for Big Edie that she needed, including a bedpan. I think it was too difficult to use, as Big Edie really couldn't move around that much. The bedsores remained. A doctor from the Medical Group suggested a prescription to put on them, and Big Edie would only allow

Doris to do it. She didn't keep her promise to Jacqueline; she had never been seen by a doctor or nurse.

About 4:00 AM, Big Edie phoned and talked with Doris a while. She was lonely.

Saturday, August 21, 1976

This afternoon, I read palms at a gathering in Wainscott, a luncheon given by Arthur Williams. I analyzed Halston's hands and other celebrities.

Doris and Peter attended a party at Tony Duke's in Boy's Harbor. It's only a stone's toss from Doris's house.

Monday, August 30, 1976

Doris and I met Joyce Egginton at 1:00 PM in Sundae's soda place. She is a writer from the London newspaper *The Observer*. We had grilled cheese sandwiches. She gave each of us a copy of *The Observer* from Sunday, August 22nd. She had one for the Beales, too. Edie had talked with her over the phone. The article was a full page! It's titled, "Love and Frustration at Grey Gardens," but it's an excellent write-up, nothing degrading. Ms. Egginton described Little Edie, Doris, and me as "middle-aged, well-bred, bohemian types." I would have preferred "middle-aged" deleted, as we don't feel we belong to a certain age group.

September & October 1976

Wednesday, September 1, 1976

While Doris and I were at Grey Gardens, today, Little Edie gave me the Tarot deck that Jacqueline had given her. The back of the interesting cards looked most occult and rather dangerous with an all-black background, a snake design on top.

It hardly seems possible, but the horrible fleas are worse, and cats have died from them again. Poor Black Cat appears moth-eaten and unhappy.

Little Edie said the oil burner had gone off so there was no hot water. Sometimes during the summers, Edie believes it's fall, and likes to turn the heat on. She intended to phone Schenck's right away. We left.

Big Edie phoned Doris around midnight. She said, "I need Edie! She's not here!"

Instead of going over there, I told Big Edie that I had a plan, and would keep calling on the telephone and not for her to answer it. Big Edie thought it was a good idea and to "do it."

After much ringing, Little Edie picked up the receiver. The trick had worked! Then we all went back to sleep at Duke Drive.

The next day, Big Edie said that we saved her life last night, and Little Edie didn't seem bothered by our persistence, since I told her it was better than our arriving at their house and banging on the front door. However, if she "didn't answer the phone, then Doris and I would get dressed and soon be on our way to wake her up!"

After that, Little Edie answered her mother, but Big Edie would still telephone Doris any hour of the night when she was uncomfortable or nervous, and just chat a while.

Sunday, September 5, 1976

We didn't drive to the Beales' today, as Muffie Meyer was expected at Grey Gardens.

Little Edie phoned about three times to tell us that a rat was in the middle of the room and she was busy getting rid of it.

Not Muffie, a real rat.

Saturday, September 18, 1976

The month of September slowly passed. Since the rolling chair accident of July 6th, it had seemed to me like a private plane crash on a hidden plateau of Mrs. Edith Bouvier Beale, with Doris Francisco carrying emergency items to the beloved victim until help came. No help ever arrived until this afternoon, when a podiatrist, a foot specialist, walked into the disaster area.

He really couldn't do much. Big Edie was still unable to move from the bed, and Doris had told me that the bedsores on her derriere were becoming ulcerated. Doris had also talked to Nancy Tuckerman about it and was trying to prevent the bedsores from getting infected, but Doris knew it would be a losing battle without a change of environment. On the telephone, the Beales minimized the situation and conversed as if everything were all right. This was "the Plaza Hotel suite cover-up" attitude. They were always worried about money and the grocery bill, and kept trying to get a check from the Maysles, but they never did. David and Al now had other films on their minds, new work to do.

The podiatrist managed to trim Big Edie's toenails, and, while doing this, he told her that she should have a doctor. He had said that Doris had been doing the right thing by bringing ice every day for the bruises and swelling, but Big Edie could have a chipped leg bone and should have x-rays taken. He could see that something was wrong, but he was not qualified to diagnose it.

Little Edie explained to us why they had decided to have a podiatrist in Grey Gardens. "Because he isn't a doctor! He couldn't upset Mother and me by ordering an ambulance. He has no authority to do anything, but he might know about bone or leg infections."

Monday, September 20, 1976

I mailed a note to Jacqueline telling her about the arrival of the podiatrist and the reasons the Beales wanted him.

I wrote Jacqueline information about Big Edie's condition. I never mentioned their money problems, as Jacqueline had said she would pay all medical expenses when she telephoned to ask her aunt to have x-rays taken.

Friday, October 1, 1976

It is cloudy and cool today. Doris talked to the Beales on the phone this morning and she told them that their film will play at the Old Post Office Cinema again on October 6th. They didn't know. Doris discovered it yesterday evening when we went to the theater to see John Wayne's picture *The Shootist*. The manager, Carol, mentioned it.

This afternoon, after stopping for the Beale mail, we drove into the grounds of Grey Gardens. I talked with Little Edie in the kitchen while Doris went upstairs. Edie wants to attend the showing of their film here, and I do hope she will be able to. Doris said she will stay with Big Edie.

On our way to the car after being locked out, Doris noticed an odd round brown thing growing or sitting on the grass near the back driveway entrance. We walked away from the car to look at it. *Terrible* looking; it made me feel ill! Doris even found another, larger one, and she hit it with a stick! We drove home and I phoned Jack Helmuth to tell him.

Tuesday, October 5, 1976

MRS. EDITH BOUVIER BEALE'S BIRTHDAY

It was pouring rain this morning. Doris and I talked with Big Edie on the telephone as soon as we finished our coffee. Little Edie said to appear for her mother's birthday party at 4:00 PM. No one else was invited, except Brooks would be there. We didn't tell the Beales, but Doris and I had to attend a funeral service at Williams' Funeral Home on Newtown Lane at 2:00 PM. A friend of Doris, and we thought it too depressing to allude to at this time. We arrived in the "Chapel" at 2:00 PM and Mr. Williams, the owner, said hello to us. We signed the guest book and sat down. It was too warm in the room and there were too many flowers. It made me feel short of breath.

We drove to the Cedar Lawn Cemetery for a short service there and then back into town. We had a few things to do at the last minute for Big Edie's 81st birthday.

It stopped raining as Doris and I drove into the grounds. Little Edie opened the door, and seemed in an unusually good mood. Brooks was smiling, too. We all went upstairs into Big Edie's bedroom. Brooks had been working hard, cleaning for the party. Big Edie gave Doris and me a cheerful greeting. She looked glamorous with her makeup on and an attractive silk shirt. Today she would be the gracious, talented hostess, without problems to trouble her guests. It was *her* birthday! The cats were roaming around with pleased expressions, jumping on and off the bed.

Before we sat down, and before Big Edie opened our gifts, she announced, "I have a present that I ordered from Brill's. Brooks picked them up for me. Give the girls their gifts, Edie. One is yours. Give Doris and Lois a package." Big Edie appeared serious as we opened the wrapping paper. She had given each of us a pair of identical black dress gloves. "Put them away," she said. "It's still too warm to wear them now, but you'll be able to soon."

We wore brown coats in the winter, some of the time, Doris wore her sky blue jacket, and Big Edie knew it. We found out later from the saleswoman at Brill's that "Mrs. Beale particularly asked for black."

Brooks, having given us the gloves as requested, served ice cream and cake.

Doris sat in the rolling chair near the bed. There had never been anything wrong with the red "run about."

We sang Happy Birthday. Big Edie appeared pleased and said she loved the presents we gave her.

The telephone rang. Much to Big Edie's delighted surprise, it was her sister Michelle on the line. Shortly, Big Edie insisted that Doris talk with her, and she did.

Later, Michelle's twin sister, Maude, phoned East Hampton. Once again, after chatting a while, Big Edie asked Doris to talk with Maude. It wasn't that Big Edie didn't want to chat with her sisters, it just seemed important to her that Doris converse with them.

The twins had mailed gifts and we had a great time exclaiming over them. Maude or Michelle even sent a coat!

Before Doris and I left Grey Gardens, Big Edie said, "It's the best birthday I ever had."

She always said that.

Wednesday, October 6, 1976

The movie *Grey Gardens* started playing at the Old Post Cffice Cinema again. It was uneventful. Only a few people attended.

Little Edie never left her Mother's house. For some reason, I don't think she wanted Doris and Big Edie talking together for any length of time.

Monday, October 11, 1976

Columbus Day

Yesterday evening, Doris phoned Anthony B. Duke about Carter's campaign here. During the conversation, she mentioned a painting I had recently finished of Jimmy Carter. Tony said for me to write Mr. Carter a note about it and he would see to it that the note would be received. This morning, I read the letter I had written. Doris liked it, and enclosed a note she had penned.

My painting of Jimmy Carter.

The Beales phoned. A holiday today and they needed food. The Newtown wouldn't deliver. Doris and I quickly left Duke Drive for Grey Gardens. We picked up Big Edie's glasses, which were broken, and drove into town. I went to Dr. York's and had the glasses repaired, while Doris shopped in the I.G.A. for a long list of groceries. We mailed the envelope to Tony Duke, picked up the mail, and returned to the Beales. We remained a long time in Big Edie's room. I think something happened there last night; I don't know what.

Tuesday, October 12, 1976

This is the last night for the Beales' movie in East Hampton. Sad…

Big Edie was not well. She phoned us because she couldn't find Edie. Asked Doris to come over, but before we could leave, Little Edie called and said not to, that everything was all right.

Friday, October 22, 1976

We talked with the Beales this morning. They need cash badly. Big Edie was upset about the grocery bill. They can't charge anymore; they have to pay each time the Newtown delivers.

Little Edie told us, "I'm busy getting a nightclub act ready. I have three songs. God! I've got to practice! By the way, Mother has the green and white Carter button pinned on that you all gave her."

November & December 1976

Wednesday, November 3, 1976

Doris got up at 5:00 AM. She was excited that Jimmy Carter had won the election. I had a cup of coffee with her and it was a happy morning.

Around 7:00 AM, Big Edie phoned, and in a very sexy voice said, "I've got Georgia on my mind... I've got Georgia on my mind..."

We knew Big Edie knew that Carter had won! She didn't even say good morning first, just a pleased, low sexy tone, "I've got Georgia on my mind..."

Sunday, November 7, 1976

LITTLE EDIE'S BIRTHDAY

Doris and I arrived at Grey Gardens at 3:00 PM, with gifts for Edie. We went into the bedroom, but there wasn't a party, and we didn't stay long. Big Edie seemed tired. We could well understand. The strain of never leaving the bed and the ulcerated sores were starting to take their toll. How she longed to go out on the porch! Brooks had tried to place Big Edie in the rolling chair, to lift her, but it caused too much pain, she said.

Doris and I continued to do all that we could during the month of November.

The house was starting to have a "dead look."

Saturday, November 27, 1976

I received a note from President-elect Jimmy Carter this morning. It was mailed from Plains, Georgia. "To Lois Wright; We have received your gift, a portrait. Rosalynn and I deeply appreciate your thoughtfulness. Your friendship and support are very valuable to us. I will do my best never to disappoint you. Sincerely, Jimmy." I was pleased.

Sunday, November 28, 1976

Bouvier Beale's two sons were at Grey Gardens today. Little Edie allowed them to go upstairs, but the two young women with them remained on the front porch.

This evening, Big Edie talked with Doris on the phone about Peter's going back to boarding school tomorrow. Big Edie even cried, as it reminded her of the days when her own sons left for boarding school and college. Doris was also sad. After the call, Doris set the alarm as she would have to get up early to drive Peter. Big Edie was worried about the trip, and Doris couldn't get back until nightfall. However, I would remain here, in contact with Grey Gardens.

But Doris and Peter couldn't leave Monday morning.

By 2:15 AM, the house on Duke Drive was engulfed in flames! Around 2:00 AM, Doris woke Peter and me up. I was sound asleep until I heard Doris calling, "Peter! Lois! Fire! There's smoke in here! Lois!" I opened the bedroom door to find Doris in the hall. There was smoke everywhere and a strong odor of something unusual. Doris, standing in her robe and slippers shouted, "We have to leave right away, don't just stand there! Lois! Peter! We're going now! Lois! *Are you coming?!*"

I felt Black Jack, Doris's cat at my feet, and picked him up. He was born on May 19th, Big Edie's brother birthday and was most unusual. We all walked out the front door. Doris had found that the telephone was dead.

I had my robe and slippers on and Peter was dressed. He ran to the next door neighbors to phone the fire department.

It was raining. Doris and I were standing on the small front porch until Doris heard a tick, tick sound from within. I still had Black Jack in my arms. "The house may blow up," Doris said softly. "Let's walk to the next house, where I told Peter to run to." We went inside. The fire department had been called. Before the fire department and police arrived, flamed were shooting into the night sky from the roof. Our throats felt very dry, and someone gave us Coke to drink, and then made coffee.

The remainder of the early morning hours was spent at another house near Wainscott, a friend of Doris, who had driven to the neighbor's house and picked us up. We had to walk quite a ways in our robes to her car as the road had been sealed off except for fire trucks and the police. The fire chief told us we would have been dead in another four minutes from smoke inhalation if we had remained sleeping.

Doris Francisco requested that the arson squad investigated the cause of the sudden fire.

Doris appeared to be calm, but I knew she was quite shaken by the shock of the terrible event. About 5:00 AM, Doris telephoned Big Edie, and I was glad she did. Big and Little Edie were already upset. Big Edie had awakened in the night and knew something frightful had happened to us. She woke Little Edie up and was waiting for our call. Big Edie was crying, this time for a different reason than earlier. She wanted to know if she could help us, if we needed clothes or anything. We said no. Doris and the Beales talked a long time until Doris felt better. I went to sleep on the couch for a while.

Later, Doris, Peter, and I were driven to another friend's house on David's Lane, East Hampton, René Jackson's studio, and we all spent the night there. After that, Doris and I moved into separate houses in East Hampton as it was more convenient for us since Peter was staying. He never left for school because of the fire.

Thursday, December 2, 1976

According to today's *East Hampton Star*, "the fire was out by 4:50 AM. The house was gutted."

Monday, December 13, 1976

Doris and I have been to talking with the Beales on the phone every day, and we have driven to Grey Gardens, but Big Edie's condition was rapidly deteriorating and Little Edie seemed to want privacy. Big Edie didn't, and called for Doris often to come over and help her.

We were getting discouraged. Doris talked with Father Huntington about Big Edie, but no one had any answers. It was tragic and on my mind all the time.

The weather had turned very cold. Little Edie talked about the winds pushing at the old house. Brooks was working there, cleaning and plugging rat holes. Little Edie commented, "The raccoons are angry about the cold, they made it known. One bit me. Of course, he didn't mean to."

Saturday, December 18, 1976

In the early evening, Doris went to church. She prays a great deal for Big Edie. I do also, but not in church… at home.

Tuesday, December 21, 1976

I wrapped all the Beales' Christmas gifts and mailed their cards.

Wednesday, December 22, 1976

I wrote on a Christmas card to Jacqueline that the Beales had received her package, and I had brought it to them. It was a book about Russia.

Thursday, December 23, 1976

I drove to Grey Gardens and went upstairs to Big Edie's room. She didn't look well. I left my presents for them. Big Edie gave me a gift she had wrapped in bed. Little Edie said, "It took Mother quite a while."

Big Edie's room had been so cold that she had to charge a small electric heater from the East Hampton Hardware store to Jacqueline. Brooks had just recently brought it in.

Friday, December 24, 1976

CHRISTMAS EVE

Doris's cat Black Jack died. A pack of dogs… it was horrible.

Doris drove to the Beales, and they told her how upset I would be when I found out about Black Jack. Doris felt terrible… we loved Black Jack.

Saturday, December 25, 1976

CHRISTMAS DAY

Christmas Day was very quiet.

Friday, December 31, 1976

New Year's Eve

I hardly realized it was New Year's Eve. I retired about 11:00 PM, very worried about Big and Little Edie. I was upset about Big Edie. I even felt sorry for myself and Grey Gardens.

JANUARY 1977

Sunday, January 16, 1977

The Beales were having frightening and depressing trials with the oil burner. I have been talking with them every day and so has Doris. We have been driving over when something was needed.

This has been a frigid, icy month and produced many problems for the Beales. Plumbing and heating emergencies, grocery bills, and Brooks's bill all stressed Big Edie, in addition to the strain of her own worsening condition in bed. Grey Gardens appeared to be "coming apart at the seams."

The wind and cold was a constant companion. Little Edie remained with her mother all the time.

Monday, January 17, 1977

Big Edie remembered her wedding anniversary and my mother's and phoned to chat about it, as she always did.

Saturday, January 22, 1977

After stopping at the I.G.A, Doris and I drove to Grey Gardens. It is sad there. There is water all over the dining room floor. Pipes are broken from the cold. We went into Big Edie's room. Big Edie is very weak and the heat is not working right. The Beales have an electric heating unit from the hardware store, but I noticed a lack of oxygen in the small, closed room. However, we remained quite a while and left when Big Edie tired. She said goodbye to us and closed her eyes to rest. Big Edie must have a strong heart, but her endurance is exhausted.

Sunday, January 23, 1977

I talked with Little Edie on the phone. She said her mother intended to telephone Nancy Tuckerman about conditions at the house. They will need a check for repair work.

Monday, January 24, 1977

Snow is still on the ground, and there is another storm warning! I talked with Edie again. She told me that they had phoned Buddy Bouvier in New York City about the head and water pipes instead of Nancy Tuckerman. I wonder what he will do. Perhaps he can get a plumber; the Beales can't get one!

Tuesday, January 25, 1977

I heard that Bouvier is sending a plumber. We are all glad of that!

Wednesday, January 26, 1977

The heat is off at Grey Gardens! Extreme weather conditions and snow are expected and a continued drop in temperature. I telephoned Little Edie. Her feet were nearly frozen from the cold. There is no heat there at all! One electric unit heater was going, placed right next to her mother's head. The plumbers arrived and are working on the pipes now. At 7:00 PM, I phoned again. Little Edie told me that her brother Bouvier insisted that they leave Grey

Gardens and go to the Huntington Inn on Main Street. Edie didn't bother to tell him that it's closed for the winter, as Big Edie said she wouldn't move anywhere except to Doris's house.

Thursday, January 27, 1977

I phoned the Beales. The baseboard heaters are working, but the house is still cold because of the awful weather, the winds, and the great drafts in Grey Gardens. Doris and I drove over with some things this afternoon: a suitcase, a heating pad—they can't use electric blankets because of the cats on the beds—and a few other items. Brooks unlocked the front door for us. The house *is* very cold. The heaters were only lukewarm. Big Edie still has the hardware store heater a few inches from her. She thanked Doris. We wanted to take her to Doris's house, but she refused to move from her bed.

Friday, January 28, 1977

The Beales have been in contact with the Medical Group. However, they do not want a doctor to appear there.

Saturday, January 29, 1977

Little Edie telephoned and wants us to come over. Said Big Edie needs Doris, said the bedsores were bothering her and she thought Doris could help her. The doctor at the Medical Group had phoned in a prescription to the drug store for them. Big Edie will not even allow her daughter to put medication on the sores. We arrived as soon as possible. Brooks let us in and then left to get the prescription. The house was cold… The hardships this winter are just too much. I am frightened. Big Edie could have blood poisoning. She was most uncomfortable. Doris managed to help her, but she desperately needs a doctor. Big Edie could die.

Sunday, January 30, 1977

I am in such despair. Big Edie is very, very ill and should have a doctor.

Monday, January 31, 1977

At last, Dr. Rowe came to Grey Gardens to see Big Edie in her bedroom, but I fear he's too late. Dr. Rowe informed them that, "Mrs. Beale should be in the hospital within an hour." The Beales said no, preventing the doctor from calling an ambulance, as he wanted to.

Night; I know that Big Edie is dying. Doris talked with Father Huntington. We are alarmed that septicemia will set in, or has already.

February 1977

Tuesday, February 1, 1977

Big Edie's condition is worse than yesterday. Little Edie asked Doris if she could drive her mother to the hospital. I don't see how it could be possible, but Doris said she would. However, Big Edie said that she wasn't ready to go, but they are excited and frantic.

Doris telephoned Father Huntington and talked with him about it.

Wednesday, February 2, 1977

This morning, Doris telephoned me and explained that Father Huntington and Sister Damian had arrived in Big Edie's bedroom. Big Edie had agreed to go into the Southampton Hospital. Little Edie wanted Doris to drive directly to the admitting office and then find Big Edie's room. Little Edie stayed at Grey Gardens; she just wanted Doris and me to go.

On our way to Southampton, we passed the red East Hampton ambulance on its return trip. Doris cried when she saw it. We parked, went in, and, after walking down long hallways, stood before the admitting office. We felt as frightened as two children.

"Where is Mrs. Edith Bouvier Beale's room?" Doris asked. "She just arrived in an ambulance."

The nurse looked at us. "Are you a relative?"

"Yes," I answered.

"Then you have to come here." She opened a door into a private office where a woman sat at a desk near a typewriter and telephone.

From that moment on, Doris and I lost our earlier childish nervousness. We sat down and soon realized that the woman, a Mrs. Hanson, knew nothing of the circumstances. She placed a form on her desk and we quickly gave her the information she wanted: Big Edie's father's name, her mother's name, place of birth, and all that. Mrs. Hanson had never heard of Mrs. Beale, the patient had been left in a double room in the old wing of the hospital. We knew without seeing it that Big Edie should be in a private room in the newer part of the building. We informed Mrs. Hanson that Mrs. Beale is Jacqueline Onassis's aunt. Immediately, Doris telephoned Nancy Tuckerman in New York. Doris told her what happened, and that a private room would only cost an additional $25 a day. Nancy said to engage the room, thanked Doris, and said she would talk with her later this afternoon.

We left the office, Mrs. Hanson guiding us to Big Edie's double room. We all walked in and were terrified when we didn't see Big Edie! It was a very tiny, ugly room, with an older woman in the next bed. A luncheon tray sat untouched on a small dresser. There wasn't a doctor or nurse nearby. Doris looked closely at what appeared to be an empty bed… and found Big Edie.

Her thin frame and her lovely face were completely hidden under the Onassis blanket. She wasn't moving and seemed to have drifted off. Doris woke her up and Big Edie recognized us. Mrs. Hanson and a nurse wanted to remove

Big Edie's sweater, but Big Edie would only allow Doris to do it. Mrs. Hanson wanted me to see the single room, to see if I approved, so we walked there and then back to Big Edie. By this time, she was on the roller-cot, with Doris standing next to her. However, Big Edie couldn't go directly to her room, number 213, as they wanted to give her a bath down the hall first. It was awful. Big Edie kept calling my name from the bath-place.

"Lois, Lois! Make them stop! They're hurting me, Lois!" I raced to the door and opened it so that Big Edie could see me. The attendants didn't like that at all. I noticed they wore blue uniforms and the room seemed rather large. One of them shut the door. I remained outside. Some nurses arrived, and then a head nurse, and finally the dunking had finished. Much to my surprise, a nurse rolled Big Edie into her new room in a hospital wheelchair. I didn't think she could sit in one. Big Edie told Doris, "The bedsores hurt. Get something for them, Babes."

Doris and I remained with Big Edie for five or six hours, until after Brooks arrived. I was looking out the hospital window when I noticed him walking towards the entrance with a small bag. "Brooks! Brooks!" I shouted and waved at him. "Brooks is here," I said to Big Edie. I knew she wanted to see him, and wanted to ask about Little Edie's being alone, without her, at Grey Gardens.

Brooks came into the room, and then went downstairs to get ice cream for everyone.

Before Brooks had left East Hampton, Nancy Tuckerman telephoned and talked with Doris again. Big Edie wanted to know who was on the line.

"Nancy Tuckerman."

"Good."

Before the New York call, I had suggested we dial Edie and place the phone so that Big Edie could say something to her daughter. They talked for about a minute, but Little Edie heard her Mother's voice.

Dr. Rowe strolled in the room this afternoon to check Big Edie and appeared surprised that she had been moved to a more expensive room. He mentioned that "Mrs. Beale should not return to her house," that she would have to go to a nursing home, after tests and treatment.

It was dark out by the time Doris and I left Big Edie. We found a stairway, a fire exit, and went down the steps and quietly walked away from the Southampton Hospital, the same hospital in which Jacqueline had been born.

Thursday, February 3, 1977

Little Edie intended to see her mother today. Father Huntington arranged for Sister Damian to drive her. Big Edie's condition is listed as "fair."

We wondered why Dr. Rowe thought his patient would leave Room 213 alive. Big Edie consented to go to the hospital because she didn't want to die in Grey Gardens. As Little Edie explained, and we all knew, if her mother died in her bedroom, the 7th Squad detectives, the police, a coroner, and the reporters would descend on Grey Gardens. After Tom "Tex" Logan succumbed there in 1963, the 7th Squad detectives arrived. With Mrs. Edith Bouvier Beale, there would be too much publicity. Big Edie didn't want that, passing on in the hospital would prevent such unpleasant activity for her daughter and other relatives.

Little Edie expected Doris and me to stay inside the old house, guarding it until her return. We arrived, and I brought my "survival kit."

The dining room was very cold. We were sitting at the large yellow painted table. It was strange to be in Grey Gardens without the Beales. The cats looked sad, but came and welcomed us. For once, there was no screwing going on by the males. They just sat and watched.

Doris and I, with the cats following, had to go up into Big Edie's room and turn the electric heater on. Little Edie suggested we do that. At last, Edie returned. Without Big Edie, the room was most depressing. The portrait of Big Edie by Herter was in the room and we often glanced at it. It is the *real* Big Edith: a diva with a high degree of merit!

Doris and I talked with Little Edie a while before we left. She approved of her mother's room at the hospital and noticed that it has a private bath with a good mirror over the wash-basin, and a large window. The room is quite attractive, comfortable, and certainly not small.

Little Edie said Big Edie asked about us.

It was very dark when Doris and I drove away from Lily Pond Lane, leaving Edie with a pensive expression, standing among her cats.

Friday, February 4, 1977

Tonight, I phoned Bouvier Beale from Ma Berman's restaurant. Doris and I agreed that we should tell him of the arrangements, and that Jacqueline would pay for his mother's private room. Bouvier was in the middle of a dinner party, but he came to the phone. However, he was in a hurry and I had to talk quickly. First I told him, "Big Edie's condition is listed as 'fair,'" then "Don't tell Little Edie that Doris phoned Nancy Tuckerman or she will *kill* us! Don't mention expenses!" Bouvier said he understood, thanked me, and would not allude to the matter when he saw his sister at the hospital.

After the call, Doris and I attempted to eat a tiny amount of food.

The daylight hours of the 4th had been occupied with the Beale crisis. Many telephone calls during the morning, and in the afternoon, we had to stay at Grey Gardens once again. Little Edie left with Brooks for the hospital, and didn't return until evening. I gave Edie two dollars to buy ice cream. It would be the last time I would ever treat them to a dish of it.

Doris and I waited. The house and the cats waited. We all felt all the cold around us. We went upstairs.

The phone rang. It was Little Edie in room 213. Big Edie wanted to talk with Doris, but she was so weak, all she could say was, "I can't do anything, Babes… I can't do anything."

Saturday, February 5, 1977

MRS. EDITH BOUVIER BEALE'S PASSING

It started to snow late last night, and by morning, we were in the middle of a severe storm.

Dr. Rowe telephoned Doris. He said that Mrs. Beale was not expected to live through the day and that we should tell Little Edie.

While I was listening to the storm warnings on the radio at home, Doris phoned, and told me about Dr. Rowe's call. "We must leave for Grey Gardens right now. I can't pick you up, Lois, the roads are too difficult. My car is stuck in the snow. I can't move it, but a neighbor is trying to free it from the drifts." Doris sounded extremely alarmed and horrified. "Get over here as soon as you can!"

Two men in an old but reliable pickup truck drove me to Doris's driveway on Dayton Lane. Doris was standing near her car while Lieutenant Ronny Adams of the East Hampton Police Department worked to move the vehicle. He lived somewhere nearby and Doris had phoned him. Ronny stopped to speak to the two men and then, with the efforts of all three, Doris's car was driven onto the street from the long driveway.

Doris asked me to get in, thanked everyone in a low tone, and drove slowly to West End Road. The heavy front door was unlocked and we went inside. Edie had just left with Brooks.

Doris telephoned Jacqueline at her New York City apartment. The butler informed her that Mrs. Onassis was out running, but that he would give her the message when she returned. Shortly, Jacqueline called Doris at Grey Gardens and they talked a long time.

Little Edie called later. "Mother's gone," she said.

Doris wept a little and looked sad. I felt a great loss.

After Doris recovered, she called Jacqueline to tell her. Jacqueline had been at home, waiting near the phone for updates.

Brooks came in later, followed by Little Edie and Bouvier Beale. He had arrived at the hospital room minutes after his mother had passed away. Little Edie and Brooks were alone with Big Edie when her spirit left her body. Bouvier could only make arrangements with the hospital and Williams' Funeral Home. He had missed speaking to his mother.

While Brooks boiled water for coffee, Little Edie, Bouvier, and I sat around the dining room table. Big Edie's youngest son intended to plan the funeral and asked us if we had any suggestions. Little Edie told him she would drive to the service with Doris and no one else. Bouvier wanted a private funeral. Edie wanted loads of flowers and a church opened to the public. Bouvier said he would have a luncheon afterward for relatives, and Doris and I would be invited there.

Bouvier left Grey Gardens first, as he had to drive all the way to his house in Glen Cove and it was still snowing.

We remained with Little Edie until we discovered that she needed something to wear for her mother's funeral. As it was scheduled for Monday, Doris and I would have to go to Brill's right away before they closed. We asked Edie if she wanted to go along, if she wanted to spend the night with either of us, but she said no, and to just select some black slacks and a black sweater. Of course, Doris, Little Edie, and I would all wear the black gloves Big Edie had given us on her last birthday.

Brooks remained with Edie and they locked the door as we left the porch. The roads had been plowed, but it was difficult driving, as the snow was banked high by the sides of the road. The woman at Brill's, Helen, was surprise to see Doris and me out in such weather. We had to tell her that Big Edie died this afternoon. Doris was crying as she bought Little Edie's wool slacks and sweater.

When I got out of the car on Egypt Lane, I asked Doris to phone me when she arrived home. I was very worried about her trip to Dayton Lane. Later on, we both telephoned Edie.

Sunday, February 6, 1977

There is snow and ice everywhere. I didn't know until much later today that Little Edie phoned Doris this morning and asked her, "I know you loved my mother, Doris, dear, and I wonder if you could help me dress her at Williams'."

"Yes, Edie, I will."

"Lois can come, too, but she doesn't have to help. She might not be able to take it. It might upset her," Edie whispered. "I'll have Mother's clothes ready when you all get here. Did you buy the slacks and sweater for me?"

"Oh, yes, Edie, and I'll lend you my mink coat."

"Thank you, Doris, dear, goodbye."

Doris picked me up at my house and we drove together to Grey Gardens. I hadn't been told of the plan, as Doris really expected Little Edie to change her mind at Williams' and just give them the clothes, as anyone else would. But it didn't happen that way…

Brooks opened the front door for us. Little Edie was upstairs getting everything packed in a small carryall bag. She looked quite well with her lipstick on. I realized that going to Williams' was important to Edie because she would have to leave Brooks alone in the house. He appeared serious or apprehensive, I thought.

Doris, Little Edie, and I walked through the snow to the car. We couldn't drive into the grounds and had to park on West End Road.

Soon, we arrived in front of Williams' on Newtown Lane, where Big Edie's body had been taken from the hospital.

William's Funeral Home is owned and operated by Mr. and Mrs. Williams, who are both licensed undertakers. Mrs. Williams's father had been an undertaker in East Hampton and his daughter had inherited the business. She met us just inside the door, as if she had been waiting. I had decided to go in, as Doris said it was too cold to sit in her car. We all walked into the small office. I sat down, but soon noticed that Doris, Edie, and Mrs. Williams all remained standing.

Mrs. Williams began, "Now, you know this is highly unusual, but if you haven't changed your mind about dressing your mother, Miss Beale…"

"No, I'll do it with Mrs. Francisco and Miss Wright. No man will touch my mother!"

"Oh, I can dress Mrs. Beale. Mr. Williams wouldn't assist, don't worry about that." She tentatively held out her hand for the bag of clothes.

"No. You know the arrangements my brother made."

"Yes, Miss Beale, we brought your mother here directly from her hospital room instead of going to the basement. You realize we are *not* supposed to be in the hospital halls, but with your connections, well… we managed to do it. And, as you requested, Mrs. Beale has not been touched since the moment she died. She is still in the hospital bed sheet."

"Thank you, Mrs. Williams. Where is Mother now?"

At that point in the conversation, I stood up.

"Well," Mrs. Williams smiled at us, "We don't call it a morgue; we call it the preparation room. Mrs. Beale is in there."

Doris had the expression on her face that I had painted of her in a past life. She was ready to start and somehow Edie and I were ready. Mrs. Williams turned and led us down a hall to the rear of the building and opened a door. She seemed nervous.

Big Edie's body was lying on a table with the bed sheet covering her. It was cold in the room so we left our coats on, but I removed my black hat and gloves. They hadn't even closed Big Edie's eyes properly. We went to work removing the sheet and placing the clothes on that Little Edie had brought, including a head scarf. Doris was very helpful and capable, lovingly patting Big Edie's arms once in a while. I did what I could. I recalled that when I was in the hospital with Big Edie last Wednesday, and she asked me to move her head so she would be more comfortable, I tried to, but couldn't, and she said, "Poor Lois…" softly.

Little Edie, Doris, and I loved Big Edie, and it seemed like ancient Egypt, a preparation room for royalty. We had so much respect for Big Edie that it was as if she had been a Queen of the Nile. Time and space disappeared as we moved Big Edie to dress her. Little Edie was right; it was the correct thing to do.

Mrs. Williams asked about makeup. Little Edie said, "Yes, my mother believed women look better with makeup."

Doris thought Mrs. Edith Bouvier Beale's head appeared uncomfortable resting on an ugly white plastic base, and soon a colored towel was folded on top of it to support her head.

Mrs. Williams brought out a kit and, turning to me, said, "Would you like to apply Mrs. Beale's makeup? Here are the brushes and colors. I know you are an artist." She held the brushes and paints towards me.

"No, thank you," I answered. "I can see how accustomed you are to the tools of makeup. You should do it."

"Well, I'll tell Mrs. Williams how Mother wore makeup," Little Edie said.

Finally, we finished, and Big Edie looked glamorous again. We all stood back to look.

Little Edie seemed pleased. "Doris, darling, isn't Mother beautiful?"

"Yes," Doris replied.

"Lois, dear, you should do a death mask. Now, who can we get next? Helen at Brill's?" Edie asked.

Mrs. Williams suddenly appeared upset, although she hadn't seemed calm before.

"I don't know her last name," Doris answered.

"How about Brooks?" I suggested. "He's a black man, Mrs. Williams. You'll recognize him when he comes in."

Much to my surprise, Mrs. Williams brought out a makeup kit for black people from a closed cabinet and handed it to me. "You see, we have all the shades from light to real black."

"Yes, you do," I said and realized that she had misunderstood Edie's "who can we get next" remark. However, I didn't say anything, as we were busy thinking other thoughts.

Mrs. Williams broke the silence by asking for stockings for Mrs. Beale's feet. Edie hadn't brought stockings.

"Big Edie liked to wear socks," I commented. "Do you have any men's socks here?"

"Oh, yes." Mrs. Williams hurried to get them. She returned with a pair of men's black knee socks. Doris and Little Edie put them on Big Edie. They looked well on her.

Doris faced Big Edie and became quiet. Little Edie and I knew then it was time to pray and say goodbye to the body, and to once again meditate on the spirit. We three stood in a straight line as Mrs. Williams left the room. Perhaps she thought we might attempt levitation or something else. Anyway, after that, she didn't care to enter the coffin room with us to select a casket. We left the preparation room and returned to the office, where Edie picked out a gray cloth coffin from a trade book.

Then, Mr. Williams came downstairs and talked with Doris and Little Edie about the location of the grave in the Bouvier plot. He also mentioned that the burial couldn't take place until Tuesday, due to the heavy snow and thick ice. Too difficult to dig.

Little Edie, Doris, and I got into the car and left for Grey Gardens. Brooks was waiting and opened the door. Edie asked him if he wanted to go right to Williams' now and see her mother, and that he had to leave immediately, as Mrs. Beale "hasn't been embalmed or anything." Brooks didn't want to go.

The casket would be closed on Tuesday. Big Edie was to remain on the table in the preparation room until then. In privacy.

Monday, February 7, 1977

Doris and I drove to Grey Gardens and went upstairs into Big Edie's room. Little Edie had left the door unlocked for us. She had been talking with her brother Bouvier. *The New York Times* and *Daily News* both carried long obituaries about Mrs. Edith Bouvier Beale. It was also on TV.

We were here today, not only to comfort Edie, but also to help select one of the old records Big Edie had made years ago. Little Edie wanted her mother's lovely, trained voice to be heard singing in the church at the funeral, and she had phoned Father Huntington to come to take the record away with him.

Little Edie was busy going through the dusty stack of records and had her outdated player on the night table.

Father Huntington and Sister Damian arrived on time. Edie played a few records and we all agreed that the song "When We are Together" would be appropriate. We felt a bittersweet sadness listening to it. Father Huntington and Sister Damian soon left.

We heard that Jacqueline and Lee will attend their aunt's funeral tomorrow, and Phelan Beale of Oklahoma City, Big Edie's older and adored son, will fly here. She had mentioned often how well Doris and Phelan would get along. She knew how much I liked Bouvier, and used to tease me about it. He resembles his mother and has a quick wit.

Little Edie asked Doris to arrive tomorrow at 10:15 AM, and then Doris and I left.

Edie carefully put her mother's records back.

Tuesday, February 8, 1977

MRS. EDITH BOUVIER BEALE'S FUNERAL

It was a clear, cold morning, with snow covering the ground.

Doris arrived at my studio on Egypt Lane about 10:00 AM and I got into her warm car. As we parked on West End

Road, Doris noticed two men standing on the porch. "It's Al and David Maysles," Doris murmured. "Look how oddly they're dressed."

We walked towards the front door and they watched us intently. It was bold of them to be here. Bouvier couldn't stand them and said he suffered greatly from the movie. Also, the "Nasals," as he called them, never sent Big Edie money for the grocery bill as they had promised on the telephone. David had on a long, purple antique overcoat cut in a military style. Al wore an old overcoat that appeared to have been lifted out of a trash can, with a rope tied around the middle! They looked very poor.

Brooks opened the heavy door and Doris and I stepped inside. "I'm not letting them in here," Brooks told us. "Mrs. Beale wouldn't like it."

"That's right," Doris answered.

Little Edie appeared, and Brooks helped her into the lovely mink coat the Doris had brought for her.

The Maysles were still standing on the porch. "Don't allow anyone inside, Brooks!" Little Edie ordered as we marched towards the car.

I knew he wouldn't.

Doris parked near the front of the Most Holy Trinity Church. We were early.

Little Edie seemed eager to leave the car. There were small groups of people standing around, and the press was parked across the street. Edie looked at the reporters and opened the door. "I would like some air, Doris, dear."

We knew Edie wanted to be seen alone and stoic when the photographers approached her. However, out of deference, no doubt, they stayed away.

Bouvier arrived with his wife and three sons and we were standing in the street when Doris and I met them.

There wasn't a police officer in sight, and one never appeared. Odd.

We were introduced to Phelan Beale. I had met his daughter Michelle years ago.

Big Edie's twin sisters, Maude and Michelle arrived, and Jacqueline and Lee. The photographers were suddenly everywhere. Someone suggested that we all go inside the church.

Halfway up the sidewalk to the door, I met Jacqueline. We both seemed to be alone at that moment. I couldn't help but notice that her large, brown eyes blazed with intelligence coupled with compassion, the two traits she had employed with her "Auntie Edith" and Little Edie.

We turned and remained together until we had both entered the church.

After waiting a while in the rear of the building, Mr. Williams and his assistants, or perhaps some church assistants, led our group down the aisle to the right pews.

Doris and I sat in the Bouvier section, and, of course, Edie and her brothers were in the front pew. Little Edie wouldn't let the Maysles attend the grave service or the luncheon and they had to stand at the back of the church.

Father Huntington conducted an impressive and beautiful service. He explained about the record Big Edie had made and that we would all hear it. There was a complete absence of any other sound except the scratches on the old recording and Big Edie's charming voice singing "When We are Together." She had such feeling. It was thrilling but oh, so sad. Or was it so sad? For we would all be together someday, and happy, as Big Edie promised. The record kept us from leaving the church in that dreadful funeral mood.

Father Huntington gave communion to the close kin sitting in the pews, except Jacqueline and Doris walked up to receive it. I remained in meditation, without the benefit of the Holy Water. So, too, did Bouvier.

The service was over. I left the church alone. Doris was talking with Jacqueline and they walked to the curb together.

Little Edie, Phelan, and I slowly got into Doris's car. The Maysles came over to us but left right away. Edie said they couldn't go to the graveside service.

Mr. Williams, the mortician, looked in the window and asked Doris to drive up and around another car as he wanted her to follow directly in back of the hearse.

We proceeded to do this and drove up to the cemetery. At the gates, we were stopped. Mr. Williams informed us that we were to be the only car allowed in, and then waved us on.

During the drive, I realized that Big Edie's thinking about Phelan and Doris was correct, that they did seem congenial.

The members of the family gathered at the gravesite as *The New York Daily News* photographers snapped pictures. They were hiding in back of Father Huntington where they could get a clear view of Jacqueline.

It was a simple service, intoned over the gray cloth casket. It was soon over.

Once again, Jacqueline joined Doris. I noticed they were talking privately as I steered Little Edie to the car. Phelan got in.

Doris drove to John Duck's in Southampton. Upon arriving, Little Edie, Doris, and I went into the powder room. We found Jacqueline doing just what Edie would be doing, gazing intently at the large mirror. Mirror, mirror, on the wall! Who's the fairest of them all? No doubt, the Bouviers are!

Jacqueline turned towards us and, during the brief conversation, she asked Little Edie and Doris for a tape recording of Aunt Edith's record. She really wanted it, but Edie didn't like the idea.

After a long luncheon, Jacqueline and Lee left. Bouvier and his wife Chicky, Phelan and his daughter Michelle, Doris, Little Edie, and I were the last to leave the private dining room.

Doris, Edie, and I drove slowly back to East Hampton. Big Edie would have approved of her funeral. Her daughter and Bouvier had managed everything well.

As we parked on West End Road, a lone man in a trench coat was waiting in the bitter cold. He didn't have gloves on and his hands looked almost frozen. He walked to the car. "Miss Beale, I'm Bob Wacker of *Newsday*."

Little Edie, sitting in the front seat, was polite to Mr. Wacker and gave him the short interview he wanted. The newspaper man left.

We went into the old house that now seemed like an empty shell.

"I wouldn't let that reporter in, Miss Edie," Brooks said. "No one else came. Cars slowed, that's all."

"Thank you, Brooks. I'll give you extra money for staying here."

Later, Doris and I returned to the car. On the way to Egypt Lane, we mentioned what Big Edie had said to use on January 31st after Dr. Rowe had left Grey Gardens. She had phoned and asked us to come over during the afternoon and have ice cream with her.

After we arrived in the bedroom that day, Big Edie asked Doris to move the rolling chair closer to the bed and sit down. I had selected my usual chair and placed a clean newspaper on the seat. Brooks served the dishes of ice cream.

Then Big Edie suddenly exclaimed, "I love both of you girls very much! And I want you to take good care of yourselves and take care of one another." It goes without saying that Big Edie loved her daughter.

"But, Big Edie," Doris replied, "we have to take care of *you!*"

Edith Bouvier Beale didn't answer. She looked out the window and into the distance. She knew the future: that the Bouvier Angel of Death would soon appear for her.

Index

THE AUTHOR

Lois Wright currently resides in East Hampton.

Printed in the United States
143092LV00001B/31/A

9 780977 746217